Money Matter.

Syed F. Mahmud / Kaoru Yamaguchi /
Murat A. Yülek

Money Matters

Some Puzzles, Anomalies and Crises
in the Standard Macroeconomic Model

PL ACADEMIC RESEARCH

Bibliographic Information published by the Deutsche Nationalbibliothek
The Deutsche Nationalbibliothek lists this publication in the Deutsche Nationalbibliografie; detailed bibliographic data is available in the internet at http://dnb.d-nb.de.

Library of Congress Cataloging-in-Publication Data
A CIP catalog record for this book has been applied for at the Library of Congress

ISBN 978-3-631-72145-2 (Print)
E-ISBN 978-3-631-72146-9 (E-PDF)
E-ISBN 978-3-631-72147-6 (EPUB)
E-ISBN 978-3-631-72148-3 (MOBI)
DOI 10.3726/b11047

© Peter Lang GmbH
Internationaler Verlag der Wissenschaften
Frankfurt am Main 2017
All rights reserved.
PL Academic Research is an Imprint of Peter Lang GmbH.

Peter Lang – Frankfurt am Main · Bern · Bruxelles ·
New York · Oxford · Warszawa · Wien

This publication has been peer reviewed.

www.peterlang.com

Abstract

The recent financial crisis showed that the current framework of the Standard Macroeconomic Model (SMM) is flawed. It does not adequately model the interactions between the financial and the real sectors. That weakens the power of the SMM in explaining the factors leading to financial crisis and in developing policies to deal with it. The SMM can also not explain important anomalies and puzzles, such as the decline and instability of the velocity of money.

The SMM portrays banks as a simple, neutral channel reallocating society's savings to investments under the Intermediation Loanable Funds (ILF) theory. In the real world, the modern banking system functions quite differently as suggested by the 'financing through lending' (FMC) theory; banks create new money when they lend. Secondly, in the SMM, money is strictly linked to the transactions in the real side of the economy. In the real world, however, significant flows of bank created credit ("debt money") go to the transactions in the financial sector (such as mortgage loans). Therefore, any growth in debt in excess of the size of the economy is not conceivable in the SMM.

The book selectively reviews and assesses the evolution of macroeconomic thought and its climax in the "Standard Macroeconomic Model" (SMM). It presents the results of Accounting System Dynamics (ASD) simulations model that suggest that excessive creation of money "out of nothing" by banks leads to the current instability of the monetary system. This leads to booms, busts and crisis. The book also discusses how the current model can be reformed to better account for the real world and policy prescriptions, such as the Chicago Plan, that can reduce the risks emanating from excessive money creation by banks.

5

About the Authors

Syed F. Mahmud is a professor of economics at Bilkent University, one of the most renowned private universities in Turkey. He holds a Ph.D. degree in economics from McMaster University (Canada) in 1986, and has over 35 years of experience in both teaching and academic research. He has held his faculty position at Bilkent University since 1989. During his tenure at Bilkent University, he has taught many courses both at graduate and undergraduate level and supervised Masters and Ph.D theses. In recent years, his research has primarily been focused on banking and finance. Applied microeconomics, using both parametric and non-parametric econometric techniques, has been one of his leading fields of specialization. He has published many papers in leading journals of economics. He has a keen interest in developing macroeconomic models based on the System Dynamic Approach and using it to evaluate the workings of alternative banking proposals, including equity-based financial systems.

Kaoru Yamaguchi is Director at Japan Futures Research Center. He holds a Ph.D. degree in economics, University of California, Berkeley (1985). He held academic posts in the USA at California State University, Hayward, the University of San Francisco, the University of Hawaii, Manoa, and then in Japan at Osaka Sangyo University, and Doshisha University (Business School) in Kyoto. He was visiting scholar at Sloan School of Management, MIT (1998, 1999), Hawaii Futures Research Center, University of Hawaii (2001), Haas School of Business, University of California, Berkeley (2003), and Victoria Management School, Victoria University of Wellington, New Zealand (2009). He served as the president of the Economics Chapter of the System Dynamics

Society (2008) and received the Advancement of Monetary Science and Reform Award from the American Monetary Institute (2010).

Murat A. Yülek is a professor of economics at Istanbul Ticaret University and the Director of the Center for Industrial Policy and Development. He is also a partner at PGlobal Global Advisory and Training Services Inc. Previously, he served as Vice Rector and Dean of the Faculty of Business Administration at THK University. He has also served as member and chairman of several boards of directors, as well as CEO of financial and non-financial institutions. He has taught at various universities, including Georgetown University and served as consultant at the World Bank, Islamic Development Bank and UNCTAD, among others. These responsibilities have exposed him to various development issues, and he has published widely in that field, as well as books and articles on economic and financial development. He holds Ph.D. and M.A. degrees in economics from Bilkent University, an MBA degree from Yale University, an MSM (management) degree from Boston University and a B.Sc. degree (mechanical engineering) from Boğaziçi University.

Acknowledgements

We would like to express our deepest thanks to Mr. Syed Imaduddin Qadri for his continued encouragement and support in writing a book on this topic. This book has also benefited from discussions with various academics and practitioners. We would like to thank Yokei Yamaguchi for complementing and contributing to research work on ASD modelling. We also thank Mustafa Resit Bulut for his tireless assistance in the preparation of charts. Kadriye Baş and Syed Shahid Mahmud also provided valuable assistance.

Preface

The so-called Great Moderation that continued from the mid-1980s until the global financial crisis led some economists to believe that the end of history in macroeconomics was reached. The crisis reversed that belief, however, showing economists that important aspects of macroeconomics, especially modelling of the monetary and financial sector, need to be revisited.

This forms the primary reason why this book has been written. The book selectively reviews and assesses the evolution of macroeconomic thought and its climax in the "Standard Macroeconomic Model" (SMM). After the Great Depression in 1929, the macroeconomics that was dominated by the Classical doctrine based on the belief of self-induced balance of supply and demand through free market forces paved way to the Keynesian revolution highlighting the importance of government intervention to counter deficiencies in aggregate demand. However, this ideological shift also did not last for too long. Several decades later, due to high inflationary trends, the New Classical economics re-emerged backed with the notions of rational expectations and monetarism. The role of government in the economy was again downgraded and neoliberalism backed up by the "New Consensus Theory" resulted into the birth of the Dynamic Stochastic General Equilibrium (DSGE) family of models that form the SMM today.

The general equilibrium framework of the SMM does not adequately model the financial-real sector interactions due to reasons ranging from analytical convenience to their axiomatic foundations. This limitation has resulted in a significant erosion of the explanatory power of the SMM in explaining the factors leading to and, consequently, in anticipating the financial crisis. Moreover, it led to the SMM's inability of developing policies to deal with the great recession that followed the crisis. For the same reason, the SMM could not explain important anomalies and puzzles, such as the decline and instability of the velocity of money or the lost decades of Japan and ineffectiveness of quantitative easing (QE) policies.

At the core of the shortcomings of the SMM is its inability to introduce any role of money and the financial sector. Firstly, it portrays banks as a simple, neutral channel reallocating society's savings to investments under the Intermediation Loanable Funds (ILF) theory. In the real world, the modern banking system functions quite differently. Banks create new money in the act of lending. This is done by matching both loan and deposit entries in the name of the same customer simultaneously as 'financing through lending' (FMC) theory suggests. The only constraint the banks face in their ability to create new money though credit extension concerns their expectations of profitability and solvency. Secondly, money is strictly linked to the transactions in the real side of the economy. In the real world, significant flows of bank created credit (debt money) go to the transactions in the financial sector (such as mortgage loans). Therefore, any growth in debt in excess of the size of the economy is not conceivable in these models.

Table 1. Standard Macroeconomic Model and the Real World: Some contrasts

SMM	Real World
Banks are considered neutral intermediaries between savers and investors (ILF)	Banks create new money endogenously: money is credit.
Money is strictly linked to the output of the real economy.	Money created by banks not only finances output (real economy) but also financial and real estate transactions, which do not contribute to GDP directly.

SMM	Real World
Aggregate private debt has no macroeconomic implication. Only distribution of debt matters.	Under the endogenous money perspective, aggregate private debt has macroeconomic implications: growing aggregate debt (money) is a source of economic growth but it can also contribute to financial fragility (Distribution of debt to productive and non-productive channels matters).
The velocity is supposed to be stable and the quantity theory of money is supposed to hold.	The velocity of money is not stable; it declines and is volatile.
Abstract model with micro-foundations and rational behavior cannot generate instability. Instability is caused by exogenous shocks only.	Debt-based system is inherently unstable with cycles of booms and busts. Many shocks are endogenous in the system.
Markets are efficient.	With imperfect and asymmetric information: Markets are mostly inefficient.
Money issuance by the central bank (e.g. QE) over and above the real growth of output will create inflation.	QE policies have proven to be ineffective in leading to inflation, particularly during post-crisis deleveraging process. However, the asset markets have benefited from these policies.

The implied borrowing constraint based on the ILF view of banking means that, in the SMM financial dysfunctions cannot be transmitted and asset price bubbles cannot form. The real world, however, has a repeated history of financial crises, involving cycles of booms and busts linked to the breakdown of the financial markets. It is now widely acknowledged that the current crisis has been caused by excessive credit flows to the financial sector (mostly mortgages) that contributed to

13

significant increase in financial leverage. Ultimately, servicing (i.e. paying back not only the principle but also the interest) the debt so created, has to be done by the real sector. That puts the real sector under undue pressure as liquidity is withdrawn from the transactions of goods and services to servicing the excessive debt created in the financial sector of the economy.

Interest payments are also important to understanding the underlying financial fragility inherent in the process of the inflation of the asset price bubble through credit flows to the financial sector. The asset price bubble would collapse when flows from the real sector are not sufficient to service the debt and investors are forced to sell their assets in the market, causing an ultimate credit crisis.

The results of simulations presented in the book, based on Accounting System Dynamics (ASD) model, reveal the instability of the system that allows excessive money creation by banks "out of nothing." Using the FMC approach, the book shows that the current monetary system is unstable. This leads to booms and busts and crisis. Recent failures of QE policy can also be attributed to the same system design failures.

This book also discusses how the current model can be reformed to better account for the real world and policy prescriptions, such as the Chicago Plan, that can reduce the risks emanating from excessive money creation by banks.

The crisis and the Great Recession have therefore prompted a debate about the state of macroeconomics, and many orthodox economists have argued that macroeconomics has entered a Dark Age. There is no doubt that the debate on the monetary and financial sector and its integration into a viable macroeconomic model, as well as on the viability of monetary and financial policies, will continue. We hope that the discussion in this book will contribute positively to those debates.

| Syed Mahmud | Kaoru Yamaguchi | Murat Yulek |
| Ankara | Awaji Island | Ankara |

Contents

15

List of Tables

List of Figures

Appendix to Chapter 4

Chapter 5

Abbreviations

ASD   Accounting System Dynamic
Fed   Federal Reserve Bank (USA)
FRB   Fractional Reserve Banking
FMC   Financing-through-money-creation
GM   Great Moderation
ILF   Intermediation Loanable Funds
RBC   Real Business Cycle
SMM   Standard Macroeconomic Model
SD   System Dynamic
SFC   Stock Flow Consistent
QE   Quantitative Easing

Chapter I
Introduction

The advent of the global financial crisis that started in 2007–2008 took not only millions, perhaps billions, of people by surprise, but also a host of economists, policy makers, regulators and international institutions. It was evident that reliance on the "standard macroeconomic model" (SMM) simply led to a failure to predict the crisis.

It is important to note that the crisis followed a long period of "great moderation" (Stock et al., 2002) characterized by a significant decline in macroeconomic volatility and stable inflation. Many economists believed that the history of severe economic crises had ended. For example, Olivier Blanchard (2008), the Director of Research at the International Monetary Fund, concluded that the "state of macro was good," and a "broad convergence of vision" was now achieved. Similarly, Nobel laureate Robert Lucas (2003) now believed that "things were under control" and the "central problem of depression-prevention has been solved." Another former Chairman of the Fed, Ben Bernanke, attributed the success of economic performance during the Great Moderation to improved policy making.

Is the model flawed or are we just facing a tail risk?

Following the emergence of the crisis, however, Alan Greenspan, another former Chairman of the Governors of the Federal Reserve Bank (Fed), admitted in 2008 that the mainstream approaches to the workings of the financial markets were flawed[1]. Nobel laureate Joseph Stiglitz (2011) pointed out that the SMM not only failed to predict the current crisis, but that it was unable to account for the severity of the crisis and the ensuing recession that followed.

Some believed that the SMM was still valid. For example, Governor Glenn Stevens of Reserve Bank of Australia apparently believed that the crisis was a once-in-a century event that the good model simply could not predict. While commenting on the intensity of international financial turmoil that followed the crisis, he remarked, "I do not know of anyone who predicted this course of events. This should give us cause to reflect on how hard a job it is to make genuinely useful forecasts." He identified the crisis as a "tail" outcome – "the kind of outcome that the routine forecasting process never predicts. But it has occurred, *it has implications and so we must reflect on it*," (RBA, 2008, emphasis added). Likewise, Ben Bernanke (2010) and other leading mainstream economists like Thomas Sargent and Oliver Blanchard (2010), in their "initial post-crisis" responses, maintained their position that these models have been useful during the good times and therefore these should not be abandoned simply because they could not foresee the crisis coming.

However, the crisis also led to a deep and prolonged recession. The central banks tried to support economic activity by lowering the policy rates, but the lower bound was quickly reached and policy makers could not raise inflationary expectations through Quantitative Easing (QE) initiatives.

In "reassessing the circumstances," Blanchard expressed a change in opinion:

---

1   Alan Greenspan admitted this in his testimony to the House Committee on Oversight and Government Reform of the US House of Representatives on October 23, 2008.

"How should we modify our benchmark models—the so-called dynamic stochastic general equilibrium (DSGE) models that we use, for example, at the IMF—to think about alternative scenarios and to quantify the effects of policy decisions? The easy and uncontroversial part of the answer is that *DSGE models should be expanded to better recognize the role of financial systems*—and this is happening. But should these models be able to describe how the economy behaves in the dark corners?" (Blanchard, 2014, emphasis added).

From the above, two conclusions may emerge. Firstly, the crisis is not a simple "tail" event and it is not a simple accident that the SMM failed to foresee it. Secondly, from an initial response of having no need for any major overhauling of the standard model, about ten years after the crisis, economists are starting to recognize the need to incorporate the ways financial systems work in the right manner into macroeconomic theory.

Quest for a new model?

Joseph Stiglitz (2011; words in brackets by authors), commenting on this new research strategy to bring financial constraints into the theory, argued that "the [standard macroeconomic] model is *not* a good starting point. Such Ptolemaic exercises in economics will be no more successful than they were in astronomy in dealing with the facts of the Copernican revolution."[2]

---

2   Research on several fronts has been initiated after the crisis. For example, introduction of 'financial frictions' in the DSGE models, by allowing for agent heterogeneity and bounded rationality. Another front is agent based model (ABN) and agent-based computational economics (ACE), Fagiolo and Roventini (2012) have provided an extensive survey of these models. However, as Bezemer (2011) pointed out these models are not embedded in theoretical framework.

The "Great Moderation" also came under scrutiny in during post-crisis analysis, as prevailing wisdom had earlier led many to believe that all was well with the current state of macroeconomics. As Blanchard (2014) now acknowledges: "The main lesson of the crisis is that we were closer to those dark corners than we thought." The Great Moderation *had fooled* not just the macroeconomists; financial institutions and regulators also underestimated the risks. The result was a financial structure that was increasingly exposed to potential shocks." Lawrence Summers suggested another explanation in this post-crisis debate; in his speech to the IMF, while commenting on the great recession that followed the crisis, he referred to it as an era of "secular stagnation," and in his view it had been with us for a long time before the crisis. Summers, in fact, was suggesting that the recession was there long before, but its visibility had been masked by the subprime bubble, and once that the bubble had burst, it became evident (Keen, 2014a). Similarly, Paul Krugman, another Nobel laureate, concluded that the "secular stagnation" may have started as early as 1985, masked by the rise in household debt.

In short, the crisis generated many anomalies for conventional economic theory. First, the theory failed to see the crisis coming. Second, the downturn persisted for a long period of time after the crisis. Third, the period of great moderation has been reinterpreted in light of the secular stagnation argument, casting doubt over the success of new consensus macroeconomic models.

The Quantity Theory of Money: How much does it hold and why?

There was yet another anomaly, after the 1980s, that is related to one of the key theoretical pillars linking the monetary and the real sectors of the economy: the "quantity theory of money," that is expressed simply as

$$MV = PY$$

where M stands for money stock, PY for the nominal value of GDP, and V the velocity of money.

With velocity of money stable, the implication of the quantity theory of money is that changes in the stock of money will have predictable consequences on nominal GDP. Therefore, having control over the stock of money has implications for inflation. In other words, the stability of the money-price link depends on the velocity of money being stable.

However, this relationship simply collapsed in the 1980s when a consistent and persistent trend of declining velocity was observed in most of the developed and emerging economies (Figure 3.1).

Given the importance of stable velocity in policy making, considerable efforts have been made to resolve the puzzle. But the results have not been conclusive (Stone et al., 1987)[3]. This led to some rightly arguing that the quantity theory of money "is now...one of the weakest stones in the foundation" (Boughton, 1991).

The debate on this puzzle has led many economists to discuss moneyless economic models based on a deductive approach that ignores the empirical facts (Werner, 2011).

---

3   The authors present an argument in the report that one possible explanation may be related to the specification problem. In the standard calculation of velocity, it is assumed that all money transactions are for the final goods and services produced in the economy. However, if these transactions also include intermediate and financial transactions, the velocity measure could vary according to the proportion of transactions in the real sector of the economy.

The case of Japan, although not directly connected to the present discussion, also posed major challenges to the state of macroeconomics. The banking crisis and recession that followed it had not been foreseen by policy makers. Lowering the interest rates did not help in ending the slump that has now entered its third decade.

Using the quantity theory of money to summarize the relationship between monetary and the real economies, at least in the long term, the velocity of circulation inherently symbolizes the financial sector. The monetary distortions get transmitted to the real sector through the velocity. In the SMM, the financial system is a simple neutral channel leading to stable velocity. That was not quite in line with the real world as the instability of velocity in the 1980s has shown. Economists have not needed the warning though, and it required a global financial crisis to remind them that the financial system has quite complex dynamics, too complex to relegate it to a simple channel through which money and funds flow between economic agents.

This book

Should economists continue with the SMM or should the SMM be enhanced to better explain the real world? The experience of the crisis suggests that at least some aspects of the SMM are highly unrealistic; the financial system is not adequately incorporated in the SMM.

Against this background, the book is structured in five chapters following the introduction. Chapter 2 briefly and selectively reviews the evolution of the mainstream macro-economic thought that culminated, in the 1980s, in the current "Standard Macroeconomic Model" (SMM), with the "New Consensus" and the domination of the Dynamic Stochastic General Equilibrium (DSGE) family of standard models as its main tools of analysis. The chapter then turns to the DSGE model and the shortcomings arising from the fact that it lacks a proper modelling of the complexities of the monetary and financial sector. It is argued that the DSGE models thus failed to explain the real world sufficiently and to predict the global financial crisis. The policy prescriptions derived from the SMM have also contributed to the severity of the financial crisis. Thus the DSGE model is further prone to fail to explain the state of the world and to predict future crises. Finally the chapter briefly reviews the Stock-Flow-Consistent models that may potentially overcome the shortcomings of the DSGE models.

On the premise of the previous chapter, in Chapter 3 we examine how the role of banks and the financial sector are being portrayed in the SMM and present alternative views that may shed some light in explaining the anomalies that we have identified. It starts by reviewing the economic theories that explain the money creation process. It then discusses possible reasons for the puzzling anomalies of the instability of the velocity and the nexus between great moderation and great recession. The chapter explains how these anomalies can be explained by using the concepts of the endogenous view of money, the Minskian financial instability process and balance sheet recession in the analysis.

Chapter 4 introduces the System Dynamic approach to macroeconomics and its application to the Japanese economy as a case, to draw inferences about the longstanding recession and current monetary policies that are ineffective. The Accounting System Dynamics (ASD) approach developed by Yamaguchi (2013) is then used to explain the implications of the process of money creation by banks under the alternative theories of fractional reserve banking (FRB) and financing through money creation (FMC). The simulation results of an ASD-based macroeconomic model for the FMC, which represent the "endogenous view of money" perspective, are also presented. These results can help in our understanding of some of the underlying vulnerabilities within the system which make it unstable. The current monetary system is shown to be unstable in the sense that it causes booms and busts and has led to the recent failures of QE policy. In other words, it has been demonstrated that the current system entails system design failures.

In Chapter 5, we review the viability of banking reforms proposed in the Chicago Plan by addressing some of the concerns deliberated in the book. The Chicago Plan is based on the proposals of Irving Fisher in the 1930s after the Great Depression of 1929. The simulation results show that this alternative system attains monetary and financial stability. As its by-product, liquidation of government debt is also shown to be concurrently attained. A business model of banks under the alternative system in which banks become genuine financial intermediaries is briefly discussed.

The final chapter summarizes the conclusions.

Chapter II
The Standard Macroeconomic Model (SMM):
A Critical Review

This chapter begins with a brief but critical review of the evolution of the theoretical background of the mainstream macroeconomic modelling that culminated in the "New Consensus" in macroeconomics in the 1980s. The consensus was ultimately reflected in the development of Dynamic Stochastic General Equilibrium (DSGE) family of standard models that became the main tools of the New Consensus. We call that duo the Standard Macro Model (SMM). We then proceed with a discussion of the DSGE model and its shortcomings in failing to properly integrate the complexities of the monetary and financial sectors. Preventing the model from explaining the real world sufficiently, these shortcomings played a key role in the DSGE models' failure to predict the global financial crisis. In the third section we discuss the Stock-Flow-Consistent models that may potentially provide an alternative to address the shortcomings of the DSGE models.

2.1 Mainstream macroeconomic modelling: A critical review

We begin with a brief review of the evolution of monetary economic thought from the classical economists in the 18th century to the New Consensus in macroeconomics in the 1980s[4]. With this, we aim to form a basis for further discussions in the book.

---

4   The review is heavily drawn from Xu (2011).

Classical economic thought was the belief that the forces of a market economy can ensure a self-driven tendency towards full employment. This belief was embedded in the principle known as *Say's Law,* which presumed that supply created its own demand. In other words, the process of production would generate enough income (and willingness to buy) to ensure that the output produced would always be sold in the market. Another important element was that the role of money was restricted to facilitating the transactions of goods and services in the economy, so money was "neutral." With flexible wages and prices, the aggregate supply curve was vertical at full employment; so changes in aggregate demand would have no impact on real output or employment with the only effect being on the price level. The classical doctrine and its laissez-fair policy prescription constituted the mainstream view until the time of Great Depression in 1929.

From three percent in 1929, the unemployment rate reached almost 25 percent in 1933 in the USA. The deep recession was persistent; even after ten years the unemployment rate exceeded 17 percent. The classical belief that any unemployment would be short-lived was not supported by actual macroeconomic performance. Furthermore, the classical paradigm also failed to explain the causes of the Great Depression, thus giving way to the ground-breaking thoughts of Keynes. Keynes argued that the causality ran from demand to supply, not vice-versa. According to Keynes, production decisions of the firms were based on expected demand. So the level of demand in the short-run could be inadequate to ensure full employment. As Keynes did not believe that market economy could automatically preserve full employment, he charged the central government to intervene to manage aggregate demand. He also disagreed with the classical direct relationship between the quantity of money and level of prices. Any increase in the quantity of money would lower the interest rate because that would increase the quantity of money available to satisfy the speculative motives for demand for money. Lower interest rates would raise investment and output. So, money was not neutral in his framework.

Keynes's theory dominated the macroeconomic field for several decades after the Second World War. Subsequently, Friedman was able to revive the quantity theory of money by arguing for the long-run inflationary effect of money. Money would only affect the price level in the long run. Instead of viewing agents responding adaptively to nominal monetary changes like Keynes, the Monetarist School took the view that agents act rationally. Friedman rejected Keynes's ideas about the long-run trade-off between unemployment and inflation, and, thanks to his and Lucas's subsequent work, the quantity theory of money ended up at the core of macroeconomics (Mankiw, 2006). So the neutrality of money, in the long run, was re-established.

Inspired by Friedman's ideas, and better equipped with advanced macroeconomic tools, the New Classical economists were able to launch their counter attack on the legacy of Keynes in the 1970s. The Lucas's monetary equilibrium business cycles theory, dealing with the monetary shocks, and later Kydland and Prescott's (1990) Real Business Cycle Theory (RBC theory) contributed to further developments of New Classical macro models.

In addition to these two developments, the Walrasian General Equilibrium framework had also been employed, and assumptions of "market clearing" and rational expectations were also incorporated into the New Classical Theories. This led to an overall framework with perfect microeconomic optimization, in which the New Classical School denied the possibility of market failures or involuntary unemployment. They re-prescribed laissez-faire: lowering of tariffs, quotas and regulations, which they thought could contribute to productivity downturns. By building perfectly competitive models and using supply side cycles, Keynes's interventionist approach had been refuted. The periods of high inflation between 1970 and 1980 also helped to promote the New Classical ideas. The microeconomic foundations of the approach also helped its credence in shaping the macro policies.

In the early 1980s, a group of diverse economists emerged with the objective of reviving the Keynesian traditions and their influence on macroeconomic framework. However, they concurred with the New Classical Economists on the importance of the microeconomic foundations and of a general equilibrium framework in building macroeconomic models. However, they believed that small market frictions might lead to substantial macro implications. Therefore, they considered that imperfect information and incomplete markets should be part of the inter-temporal equilibrium model.

The New Keynesians in this way were able to provide solid microeconomic foundations that allowed the possibility of wages and prices not clearing the markets. They based their formal macroeconomic modeling on the New Keynesian version of the Dynamic Stochastic General Equilibrium (DSGE) model containing price stickiness and wage rigidities. The model embraced the idea of market clearing and self-regulation of the system, while denying the role of an intrinsic effective failure of demand and focused on the supply side of the economy, which had been previously rejected by Keynes (Arestis and Sawyer, 2002).

In effect, the New Keynesians gave less priority to fiscal policy and proposed using monetary policy as the primary tool in aggregate demand management. To some economists, for example, Leijonhufvud (2009), "besides some micro inflexibility, this brand of macroeconomic theory has basically nothing Keynesian about it."

With these common views on vision and methodologies, the New Keynesian and New Classical economic ideas about monetary policy converged in the latter half of the 20th century. This convergence between the two rival camps is now known as the "New Consensus" (NC) or the "New Neoclassical Synthesis." It integrates some elements of Keynes, such as nominal rigidities and imperfect competition into the RBC general equilibrium framework (Snowdon and Vane, 2005). One of the important implications of this synthesis was the convergence of views on the pre-eminence of an active monetary policy over fiscal policy to deal with business cycles and recessionary trends. In that sense, no doubt, they were effective in designing policy after the global financial crisis. Furthermore, the belief in free market forces ensuring adjustments towards equilibrium had been restored.

Macroeconomic trends during the "great moderation" (GM) in the 1980s also helped promote the development of macro models along these lines. The US economy and the world economy underwent a long period of boom with little volatility in output. Blanchard and Simon (2001) had documented the fact that the variability in quarterly real output growth had declined by half since the mid-1980s. Well-known mainstream economists were delighted by these results and attributed this to the advancement in macroeconomic theory and improvement in monetary policy. Blanchard (2008) concluded that "the state of macro is good."

2.2 DSGE models and their shortcomings in capturing the financial sector

The main tools used by economists to reach this state of conviction were the DSGE models. Thus, in fact, a new, more important consensus among differing schools of thought than the NC was that the DSGE models (of different varieties) were the best tool to proceed with macroeconomic analysis. However, the belief that mainstream macroeconomists had solved the major problems of macroeconomics ended with the anti-climax of the momentous downturn in 2007. So, a brief look at the DSGE models is warranted at this stage.

The DSGE models are basically short-run models. They relied heavily on the process of market adjustments and believed that these adjustments would finally restore equilibrium in the short run. This conviction was founded on four simple key assumptions. First, consumers maximize their utility under a budget constraint. Second, firms maximize profits under a resource constraint. Third, markets have the built-in dynamics to restore equilibrium in response to certain external shocks. Finally, the representative agents are guided by "rational expectations."

The DSGE models do allow for short-run deviations from the steady state equilibrium, due to the presence of sticky wages and prices, adjustment costs and other exogenous shocks. However, by assuming "rational" behavior by market participants and the inherent ability of the markets to clear, DSGE models always produce an intertemporal trend towards equilibrium. In his testimony and critical review to the US Senate, Solow (2010) stated that DSGE models treat the whole economy as one single consistent person who is assumed to carry out a long-term plan which is rationally designed, occasionally disturbed by unexpected shocks, but who can adapt them in a rational manner, which is founded on microeconomic behaviour.

In one of the post-crisis working papers of the Banking International Settlement (BIS), Tovar (2008) notes that one of the crucial shortcomings of DSGE model is their inability to incorporate the financial sector properly. This exclusion is justified on the basis of the so-called "efficient market hypothesis," which states that financial markets are always cleared (Krugman, 2009). The hypothesis rests on the belief that market prices of financial assets follow the fundamentals of the markets. Consequently, aggregate financial wealth does not have any consequence to the behavior of agents and/ or to the dynamics of the economy. Cechetti et al. (2012) also argues that while constructing a theoretical structure of the economy as a whole, debt is trivial, as the liabilities of all borrowers are being canceled out by the assets of all lenders, and therefore money does not have any active role in these models. The monetary side of the economy is therefore fully constrained by the real side of the economy; money in these models is treated as a "veil," a mere unit of account that facilitates transactions of goods and services.

Godley and Shaikh (2002) show that it is the very structure of these models that prevents the integration of the financial sector into the framework. As Bezemer (2011) pointed out, any attempt to incorporate money and/or financial sectors into these models would simply undermine the models' key properties. This denies the very nature of finance, which is "leverage," in which debt claims can be created in excess of current output (Bezemer 2011).

A short summary of the features of DSGE family of models are:

1. They are based on the micro-underpinning of the individual's optimization framework;
2. They assume that the economy is either in equilibrium or it will return to equilibrium soon if disturbed by unanticipated external shocks;
3. Uncertainty is dealt with by the proposition that a rational individual can accurately foresee the future (Rational Expectations);

The shortcomings of the DSGE models from the point of view of our discussion at this stage are:

1. They treat a complex monetary market economy as a barter system;
2. Money supply is explained through a simple "money multiplier" model;
3. They fail to incorporate the financial sector—the roles of credit and debt—into the macro economy.

Stiglitz (2011) emphasizes that the current macroeconomic models do not have the capability to address the relevant policy issues at hand. Explaining that there are always trade-offs in any modelling approach, he argues that the standard approach to macroeconomics has been too ambitious, with some priorities seemingly making some wrong trade-offs elsewhere. Particularly, in his opinion, the complexities that may arise from intertemporal maximization over an infinite horizon are far less relevant than incorporating a better description of financial markets. He suggests that a future modelling approach should bring greater realism into their modelling of banking/shadow banking.

The disproportionate size of the global financial crisis gives credence to Stiglitz's criticism of the standard model, which was effectively defended by Blanchard on pragmatic grounds. The conviction of mainstream macroeconomists that they had solved the major problems of macroeconomics ended with the anti-climax of the momentous downturn in 2007.

In parallel, Claudio (2012), an economist of the Bank of International Settlement (BIS)—the central banker of the central banks—makes a serious call about the validity of the neoclassical DSGE models in policy making:

"Three themes run through the essay. Think medium term! The financial cycle is much longer than the traditional business cycle. Think monetary! Modelling the financial cycle correctly, rather than simply mimicking some of its features superficially, requires recognizing fully the fundamental monetary nature of our economies: *the financial system does not just allocate, but it also generates purchasing power*, and has very much a life of its own" (Claudio, 2012, emphasis added).

Our main conclusion; it is evident that there is a need to develop a new methodology that fully recognizes the fundamental monetary and financial nature of our economies. Traditional macroeconomic theory, and thus the DSGE model, has long ignored money and finance. This is perhaps a reflection of the conviction that either banks, debt and money are not easy to model or they do not matter. But continuing with the same simplification will end up continuing with a poor explanation of the real world.

2.3 Is a fundamental change in the SMM warranted, or should we continue with the "models for good times and models for bad times?"

The current consensus on macroeconomics is now facing challenges similar to those faced by the Classical economists during the Great Depression. Faced with the challenge, Blanchard et al. (2010) admitted: "identifying the flaws of existing policy is (relatively) easy. Defining a new macroeconomic framework is much harder." Later, he offered a pragmatic solution to the difficulty: "If macroeconomic policy and financial regulation are set in such a way as to maintain a healthy distance from dark corners, then our models that portray normal times may still be largely appropriate. *Another class of economic models*, aimed at measuring systemic risk, can be used to give warning signals that we are getting too close to dark corners, and steps must be taken to reduce risk and increase distance," (Blanchard, 2014, emphasis added). In short, what is proposed is (1) to keep the current models in use (as it will be hard to change them) and derive policy implications from them during the good times; and (2) develop and employ some other models for the management of the risk of getting close to the dark corners.

Having two different models, one for good times and the other for the bad times, could perhaps be something that can be prescribed as a short term practical measure. But as the post-crisis discussion of secular stagnation has revealed, the good times and bad times are intertwined. If the good times and the bad times are not clearly delineated, the policymaker using the model for the good times may be sowing the seeds for the visible emergence of the bad times.

2.4 Stock Flow Consistent (SFC) Models

On the periphery of the mainstream, several non-neoclassical economists have been working on "Stock-Flow-Consistent" (SFC) models. They incorporate all financial flows into the model endogenously and solve complex differential equations numerically. Thus, they have the potential to overcome the key deficiency of the DSGE models cited above. It is worthwhile to note that their approach is still in the process of development and may need some time both to get acknowledged and to find ways to be integrated into the mainstream approach.

The SFC models are primarily types of macro models that comprehensibly integrate all stocks and flows of an economy (Caverzasi et al., 2013). The approach starts with the "circular flow" view of the monetary economy, in which, every transaction of goods and services finds its counterpart in the flow of a credit/debt instrument, each flow comes from somewhere and goes somewhere (Bezemer, 2010).

These models represent the economy in terms of a balance sheet, where, by definition, liabilities and assets are balanced. The historical roots of these models can be traced back to the work of Morris Copeland (1949), who sought to find answers to fundamental economic questions, such as "when do total purchases of our national product increase?", "where does the money come from to finance them?", "when do purchases of our national product decline?" and "what becomes of the money that is not spent?" (Copeland 1949). Those questions led him to lay the foundation of an approach that enabled him to integrate real and financial flows of an economy (Caverzasi et al., 2013). Copeland introduced the quadruple-entry system, which has become one of the crucial elements in the contemporary SFC models, in which someone's inflow is someone else's outflow, based on the double-entry system of accounting.

James Tobin made a significant contribution in establishing the accounting approach in the 1980s (Bezemer, 2010). Although many of Tobin's earlier contributions were based on mainstream traditions, in the 1980s he initiated a research program at Yale developing SFC models. In these models he was able to incorporate financial and monetary policy operations and other features of SFC's consistent approach. Kalecki and Minsky have also been prominent advocates of the accounting approach.

The contemporary non-orthodox economists who have been following the SFC framework include Godley, Baker, Hudson, Keen, Yamaguchi and others.[5] Some of them were

---

5   For the theoretical papers/books outlining the SFC approach, see
    Baker et al (2005), Keen (1995, 2009), Hudson (2006), Godley

successful in predicting the crisis and have also contributed to the development of a theoretical framework based of the SFC approach. For example, Wynne Godley and others, in April 2007, made their predictions of a slowdown in growth of output to almost zero "sometime between now and 2008." In November 2007, they again forecast a significant drop in borrowing and private expenditures, with severe consequences for growth and unemployment in coming quarters (Godley and Zezza 2006). Hudson (2006) has warned about the record mortgage debt and rising debt-service payments that will divert income from consumer spending and may thus push the economy into Japan-style stagnation.

2.5 Conclusions

The NC has another key underlying consensus: the role of DSGE models as its main tool of analysis. However, the DSGE models do not capture the complex dynamics of the monetary and financial sectors. That is evidently the key reason why they failed to predict the global financial crisis. We conclude that alternative tools, which explain the real world of complicated financial flows better, are necessary. SFC has the potential to be one of them.

and Wray (2000), Godley and Zezza (2006), Godley and Lavoie (2007), Yamaguchi (2013).

Chapter III
Endogenous Money, Minskian Financial Crises and the Balance Sheet Recession: Resolving Puzzles and Anomalies

The financial crisis of 2007 brought an abrupt end to "The Great Moderation," a long period of economic stability, which had lasted since the mid 1980s (Bernanke 2004; Davis and Kahn, 2008; Gali and Gambetti, 2009). The Great Moderation not only saw unusual macroeconomic stability, but also a rise in asset prices and strong growth in credit in relation to output. Importantly, there was a marked shift of credit flows to the financial sector compared to the real sector.

Significant shifts in credits during a credit boom, from relatively low-risk, low-return investments in the real sector to high-risk, high-return ones in the financial sectors (real estate and financial assets), can increase the financial fragility of the system (Beck et al, 2012). Shifts in credit flows to the financial sector diminish its link with output growth (Tobin, 1984). In its final phases, before the bust, credit growth coupled with rising asset prices started reinforcing each other, and credit growth was no longer driven by market fundamentals (Bezemer and Grydaki, 2014, Allen and Gale, 2000).

A persistent and significant drop in the velocity of money since the 1980s has been another important trend. The puzzle of unstable velocity, which remained unresolved for a long time, also has links to developments in the credit markets that lead to recessions and crises.

The standard macroeconomic model (SMM), by not taking into account the central role of credit in the economy properly, has failed to predict or explain either the longstanding recession or the financial crisis. It ignored the role of money and the process of its creation. In the SMM, money and finance are modelled with no impact on the real economy, particularly in the long run. The mode of financing is also not accorded proper importance. For example, in the Modigliani-Miller theorem, the value of a private firm is unaffected by its capital structure. Moreover, the Efficient Market Hypothesis maintains that processes in the financial markets reflect all available information and therefore financial markets can neither cause a bubble nor have any effects on real sector growth.

Such theories rest primarily on treating money as a unit of account, linking money to the transactions of goods and services only, and ignoring the "endogenous view" of money, where money is also a form of credit. Implications of different credit instruments and balance sheet effects are ignored in the SMM.

In this chapter we aim to shed light on the possible reasons for the anomalies that have been mentioned earlier (the puzzle of unstable velocity, the nexus between the great moderation and great recession) using the concepts of the endogenous view of money, the Minskian financial instability process and the balance sheet recession.

We begin by a short discussion of the views on the money creation process in banks, as the assumptions made by different schools of thought yield diverse views about the money in the economy[6]. We then proceed to discuss the concepts of endogenous view of money and balance sheet recession, and what differences they generate compared to the SMM in explaining anomalies.

---

6 See Kohn (1988) for a detailed review of the theory of money in economic thought.

3.1. The Creation of Bank Money: A Brief Survey of the Earlier Discussion

The role of banks as financial intermediaries has been a contentious issue during different times in the 20th century. One of the oldest views supported "the credit creation theory" (or, financing-through-money-creation, FMC), where banks are considered to create money individually through accounting operations when they extend a loan.[7] The theory was dominant until about the mid to late 1920s (Werner, 2015). It was later replaced by the fractional reserve banking/money multiplier model (FRB). In this model, banks need excess reserves before they can lend money to the borrowers. The excess reserves are created, initially, through an injection of government-created "fiat money." The recipients of the fiat money can lend a fraction of it, ultimately creating credit money in the magnitude of a multiple of the initial deposit of fiat money. In this process "only" the banking system as a whole can collectively contribute to the expansion of money[8].

The FRB had considerable influence until about the 1960s (Werner, 2015). It led to the most dominant theory, the "Intermediation of loanable fund theory' (ILF), which holds banks as mere "*financial intermediaries*," collecting deposits and lending them out, acting as any other non-bank financial

---

7   MacLeod (1856), Withers (1916, 1921), Schumpeter (1912), Wicksell (1898) and Hahn (1924).

8   Aschheim (1959), Paul Smith (1966), Guttentag and Lindsay (1968), Samuelson (1948) and others. Fractional reserve banking system is mainly discussed in undergraduate textbooks; at the graduate level and in theoretical macro modeling, the financial intermediary role of banks is covered.

institution[9]. In this view of banking, neither an individual bank nor the banking sector as whole, can expand/contract money supply. The view had two broad implications for the mainstream theoretical models. First, by confining the role of banks to intermediaries, the banks can simply be ignored in the modeling. Second, the level of private debt across the economy can also be ignored, because a loan is regarded as a transfer of spending power from one individual to another. As one person's spending power goes down and another's is going up, the aggregate debt level has only distributional consequences. Consequently, in commenting on Irving Fisher's "debt deflation" explanation of the Great Depression, Bernanke wrote: "Fisher's idea was less influential in academic circles, though, because of the counterargument that debt-deflation represented no more than a redistribution from one group (debtors) to another (creditors). Absent implausibly large differences in marginal spending propensities among the group, it was suggested, pure redistributions should have no significant macro-economic effects…" (Bernanke, 2000).

3.2 The Endogenous View of Money: Can It Solve the Puzzles?

In this chapter, our aim is to investigate the key underlying limitations of the SMM approach and how this may explain its recent failures, instead of entering into a detailed discussion on different views of economists about how banks do operate.

SMM modeling is essentially based on a deductive methodology, grounded on axioms and assumptions, including

---

9 Gurley and Shaw (1960), Gutteng and Lindsay (1968), Tobin (1963) and many others. For a detailed review of literature on this subject see Werner (2014, 2015), and Vivian et al. (2015).

the "financial intermediary" role of banks. However, many practitioners and heads of leading financial institutions have supported the "credit creation theory" in general, and numerous empirical studies have verified the endogenous view of money[10]. The endogenous view of money or "credit creation theory" (FMC) basically rests on the idea that when a bank makes an initial loan to a borrower, it simultaneously creates an equivalent deposit. So, credit and money are created endogenously, independent of prior cash deposits. The bank can obtain the reserves later to meet the reserve requirements or withdrawals as needed (Fullwiler, 2013). So, the direction of the causality is precisely the reverse of what is being maintained by the current mainstream views. However, the heads of many central banks and bank professionals have supported the endogenous view of money in the past. The senior Vice-President of the New York Federal Reserve, Alan Holmes, stated that treating banks as mere intermediaries between savers and lenders was erroneous. He argued that the view "that the banking system only expands loans after the [Federal Reserve] System (or market factors) has put reserves in the banking system" was based on "a naive assumption." He argued, *In the real world, banks extend credit, creating deposits in the process, and look for the reserves later."* So, according to Holmes, banks do not need deposits in order lend and banks can create spending power by issuing loans[11]. In one of the recent Bundesbank (2009) reports about the banking system in the eurozone, it is suggested that

---

10 For example, Bank of England (2014), Benes and Kumhof (2012), Moore (1979, 1995, 2001, 2006) and many others.

11 Fullwiler (2013) describes in detail the banking model in actual practice and the endogenous money perspective on the interactions between central bank operations and banks. The

"In the Eurosystem, money is primarily created through the extension of bank credit... The commercial banks can create money themselves, the so-called giro money." Another recently published article by the Bank of England (Jakab et al. 2014), argued "the creation of gross positions with zero net principle value, but of course with a positive net interest rate that flows to the bank over time, is precisely the meaning of bank financing, the very rationale for the existence of banks" (Jakab et al. 2014).

In another article published in the Bank of England's quarterly review (McLeay et al., 2014), the conventional theories of bank lending and the process of money creation are discredited, endorsing the view that commercial banks are actually creators of deposit money which is what the endogenous money view suggests. By lending money that banks do not possess, commercial banks are in effect creating new money (McLeay et al. 2014).

The endogenous view of money has also been supported in the works of a number of other economists. Claudio (2012), in a BIS research paper, emphasized the fact that in order to make macro models relevant in policy making, the models must recognize "the fundamental monetary nature of our economies: the financial system does not only just allocate, but also generates, purchasing power." Recent empirical analysis by Basil Moore (1979, 2001, 2006) has further given credence and force to the arguments of proponents of endogenous money views. The concept of the endogenous view has been fundamental to Minsky's Instability Hypothesis (1978, 1982) and can also be found in Schumpeter's works (1934).

---

paper shows that interest on reserve balances does obstruct the functioning of monetary policy and quantitative easing may not necessarily increase it.

The lack of any role by banks and the absence of financial markets in the DSGE models has been defended on the grounds that the model was sophisticated enough, since it incorporates frictional unemployment, financial imperfections and sticky prices and wages. However, as Stiglitz (2011) and Tovar (2008) point out, such "stable-with-friction" models can mimic non-linear dynamics, but they cannot incorporate the financial causes of these nonlinearities, as they fail to model financial models in a suitable way.

As the financial side of the economy is fully determined by the real side of the economy in the SMM, money must exist in proportion to the aggregate of all transactions in the real economy. This is why the "equation of exchange" has been an important feature of general equilibrium models. Eggertson and Krugman (2012) acknowledged that while there has been a long discussion of making debt one of the major factors in determining economic contractions, there is a lack of models that address debt concerns.

In light of the discussion above, we now present some of the explanations of anomalies discussed earlier, based on the endogenous view of money. We start with the anomaly of the "declining velocity of money," as it has had severe implications for the stability of the money-price link that is central to the SMM approach. Later we will also add explanations of other anomalies, such as the protracted recession that followed the crisis, the inefficacy of traditional monetary measures and the gross failure of DSGE models to foresee the crisis.

3.2.1 Anomaly of "Declining Velocity of Money": Can the Endogenous View of Money Solve the Puzzle?

Referring back to the macroeconomic relationship between money, GDP and prices, the equation of exchange or what is known as the "quantity theory of money" is:

$$MV = PY \qquad\qquad [1]$$

In typical empirical work, some aggregate of private sector deposits, such as M1, M2, M3 are employed to represent M, the money stock. PY represents the nominal value of national income and V is the velocity of money.

Invoking the equilibrium condition in the money market, M, in effect, also represents demand for money. This fundamental relationship captures some of the key aspects of the SMM theoretical framework and underlying assumptions. With the loanable fund theory of intermediation (ILF) theory, M is taken as an exogenous variable, managed by different monetary tools of the central bank, such as open market operations and reserve requirements. Furthermore, money exists in equilibrium in strict proportion to the transactions in goods and services in the real sector of the economy.

The stable relationship, which is implied by this equation, has appeared to hold until the 1970s; however, it broke down completely during 1980s. The drop in the velocity was more consistent and profound in the developed economies (Figure 3.1). This had broad implications for monetary policy, as it implied an unstable demand for money, hence posing challenges in implementing an effective monetary policy. Given the significance of the issue, it prompted considerable efforts in a search for a solution to this puzzle.

Figure 3.1: Recent trends in velocity of money

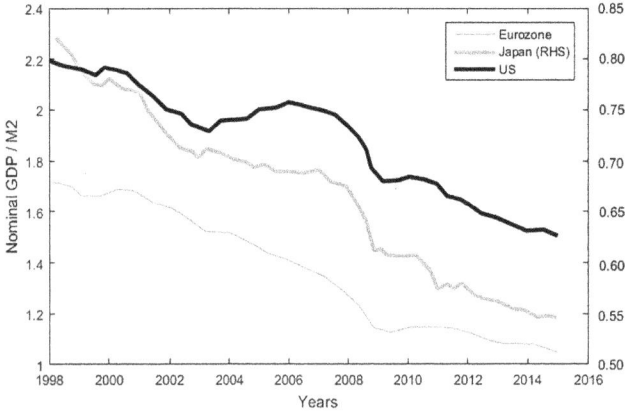

Source: Brown (2015)

One of the reports of the Federal Reserve Bank of St. Louis, dedicated to this issue, reviewed a number of explanations for the puzzling downturn in M1 velocity in the 1980s and made its assessment of the credibility of some of the explanations accounting for this behavior (Stone et al., 1987). In its conclusions, the report found most of the explanations inadequate. However, it suggested that the contributions of financial innovations and cyclical variations were among the most prominent in explaining the anomaly. According to several other surveys, financial liberalization and structural changes in the financial system in the 1980s were offered as plausible explanations (Goodhart, 1989, Goldfeld and Sichel, 1990).

Recently, Richard Werner has presented an alternative account of the anomaly by integrating into his analyses the endogenous view of money and credit flows to the financial and non-financial sectors. In his book, *New Paradigm in Macroeconomics* (Palgrave McMillan, 2005), Werner develops what he refers to as the "quantity theory of credit." The quantity theory of credit is noteworthy as it offers a simple explanation of the puzzle. Thus, it is worth expounding on the basic features of Werner's theory and presenting some of his empirical findings in support of his theory.

Werner starts with the observation that the use of some deposit aggregate in [1] may not be appropriate because only the purchasing power that is actually used for transactions should matter in the equation. The traditional monetary aggregates, such as M1, M2, M3, refer to money deposited with the banks and they reflect the potential, not the effective purchasing power; it is only actual spending that is expected to affect GDP in [1].

By defining money as private sector assets, such as deposits, it may not be clear where to draw the line among the wide spectrum of private assets. Werner proposes that this issue can be resolved by changing the focus from the traditional use of monetary aggregates to a measure of "credit creation." Total bank credit as a measure of money supply M in [1] should represent the effective purchasing power, as money is being borrowed with specific intent to be used in transactions. Another advantage of using credit aggregates is that these are available by economic sectors, providing additional information on the direction of flows. Friedman (1987) had also made a similar suggestion on the feasibility of dividing the money flows into different sectors of the economy:

"Each side of this equation can be broken into subcategories: the right-hand side into different categories of transactions and the left-hand side into payments in different form."

That de-coupling was not possible with the deposit aggregates M1, M2 and M3. Contrary to the traditional interpretation of [1], where all money is tied to transactions in the real sector of the economy, by using total credit based on the credit creation view of money, it is possible to distinguish between flows to the real and financial sectors of the economy.

Werner starts with a dichotomous credit-money circulation as:

$$C = C_R + C_F \qquad [2]$$

Where C represents total loans by the deposit-taking financial institutions, C_R represents credit flows for real transactions (such as investment and consumption), and C_F for the financial transactions (such as real estate purchases, which are not part of GDP). So for the real economy, [1] can be redefined as:

$$C_R V_R = P_R Y \qquad [3]$$

In this re-interpretation of the equation of exchange, the stock of credit money that flows into the real economy determines the nominal value of goods and services. V_R represents the stable "real" velocity of credit money.

However, with the phenomenal growth in the financial sector since the 1980s and significant flows of credit to this sector for a significant length of time, Werner makes a simple assumption that asset price adjustments also take similar form, and gives a tentative formulation of credit flows into the financial sector as[12]:

$$C_F V_F = P_F A \qquad [4]$$

---

12 We discuss more formal dynamics of the financial sector and how it may be linked to financial fragility and contribute to the building up of the financial crisis in the next section.

Taking the first differences of [3] and [4], one ends up with

$$\Delta(C_R V_R) = \Delta(P_R Y) \tag{5}$$

$$\Delta(C_F V_F) = \Delta(P_F A) \tag{6}$$

Werner (1992, 1997) shows that the widely observed velocity decline in the case of Japan is not necessarily directly linked to financial innovations or deregulation, but can be explained simply by noting the increase in money used for transactions that are not part of the real sector, i.e. asset transactions.

From [5] it follows that bank credit creation should boost nominal growth in GDP (Figure 3.1a). Similarly link between credit flows to real estate (land) and changes in the price of land is also shown in Figure 3.1b.

Figure 3.1a Growth driven by credit creation for GDP transactions (CR), Japan

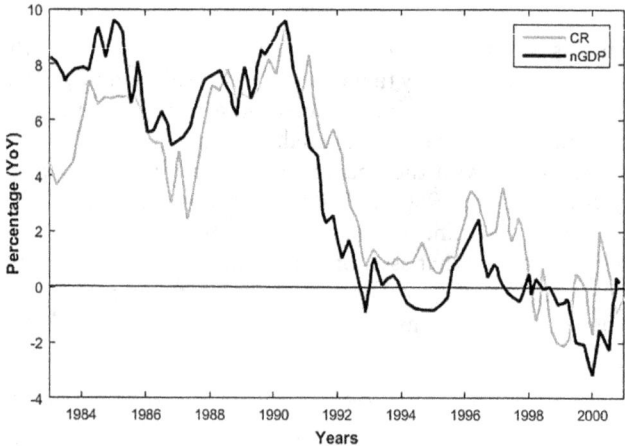

Source: Werner (2012)

Figure 3.1b Credit used for real estate transactions and land prices (Japan)

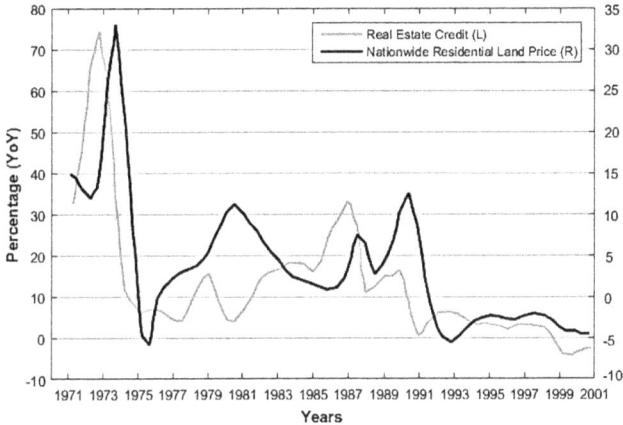

Source: Werner (2012)

In his more rigorous econometric analysis, he finds that growth in credit flows to the real sector accounts for more than 90 % of nominal growth in GDP. He also found evidence of strong Granger's one way causality, running from growth in credits to growth in nominal GDP. Also, redefining the velocity of money as in [3], an empirical test of the stable velocity of money has also been confirmed.

Similar observations have been made for the US economy (Figure 3.2). Again, the close correspondence between growth of credit to the real sector and nominal growth in GDP shows that growth in all final goods-and-services transactions requires additional money. The close correspondence with GDP, however, does not hold for the growth of total bank credit stock. Again, this highlights the fact that we may need to make a distinction between different categories of credit performing different economic functions (LSE Report, 2011). Just as credit flows to the real sector facilitate liquidity in the real sector of the economy, credit flowing to the financial sector provides liquidity for the assets markets. This is why credits to the financial sector do not follow any close track to GDP as financial transactions do not contribute to GDP.

Thus, the endogenous view of money together with the de-coupling of credit flows into the real and financial sectors provide one possible explanation that resolves the puzzle of unstable, declining velocity.

Figure 3.2a Credit to the real and property sectors in the USA

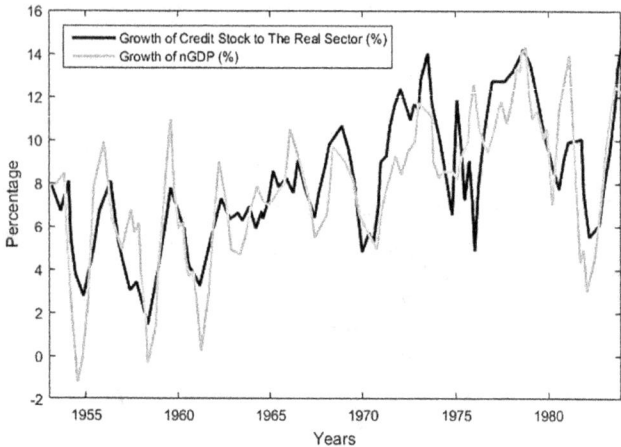

Source: Bezemer (2014)

Figure 3.2b Credit to the real and property sectors in the USA

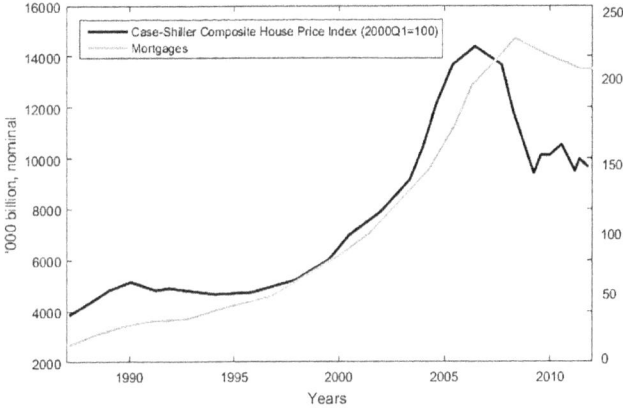

Source: Bezemer (2014)

3.3. From Great Moderation to Great Recession: The Minskian Scenario of Financial Crises[13]

The decomposition of credit flows can also be useful in explaining financial fragility (Bezemer and Grydaki, 2014). Turner et al (2010) argue that in understanding the build-up of financial fragility in the system[14], it is important to distinguish between different categories of credit, which perform different economic functions. Financial deepening

---

13 The model and arguments presented in this section have drawn from the recent work of Keen (2013). The model is based on his earlier work on Minsky's Financial Instability Hypothesis (Keen, 1995).

14 Financial fragility can usefully be defined as sensitivity of default rates to income or asset price shocks (Jappalli, 2008).

is often measured by the ratio of bank credit to GDP. Empirical work has shown significant links between this ratio and economic growth, particularly in the medium income developing economies (King and Levine, 1993; Goldsmith, 1969; Shaw, 1973; Yulek, 1998Ang, 2008). More recent work (such as Rousseau and Wachtel, 2011, Archand et al., 2012, Cecchetti and Kharroubi, 2012) contribute to financial fragility (Reinhart and Rogoff, 2009, Taylor, 2012, Jorda et al., 2011) on this association has also shown that high values of the credit-to-GDP may slow growth.

Following Bezemer and Grydaki (2014), we pose two important questions: (1) how does the relation between credit growth and output (GDP) growth change during a booming credit market? And, (2) which of these changes may turn these credit booms into credit bubbles?

As mentioned earlier, bank credits to the real sector are fairly stable in proportion to the nominal value of GDP, which indicates the size of the real economy. Werner (2005) found close correspondence between the fluctuations in credit growth in the real sector and GDP in the cases of both the Japanese (Figure 3.1) and American economies (Figure 3.2), with the ratio of credits to the non-financial sector around 100 percent between 1951–2007 (Bezemer and Grydaki, 2014). However, credit flows to the financial sector have risen significantly during the Great Moderation in the US. These flows are not taken into account in the SMM, as money is linked strictly to the transactions of the real economy. But these flows are important in understanding the finance-induced instability. As Bezemer points out, rise in debt due to credit flows to the financial sector must imply an increase in the economy's "overall leverage," that is, credit created in excess of the size of the real economy. This is reflected in rising debt to GDP ratio(s)[15]. We further expound on this point later in this section, by employing a simple balance sheet approach applied to the economy.

Keen (2011, 2013) uses a system dynamic model based on Goodwin's (1967) deterministic structural growth cycle model to explain Minsky's financial instability hypothesis, which presents an intuitive description of the dynamics of an economy from great moderation to great recession. Keen takes the streamlined financial cycle scenario developed by Minsky that starts at a time when the economy is doing well and economic growth is able to maintain low unemployment rates. The private sector of the economy is conservative in their portfolio choices with low debt to equity ratios during this period of tranquillity. This behavior is also shared by the banks, who finance low risk investments perhaps due to some system-wide financial failure in the distant past.

As the economy grows with relatively high success rates in the projects financed by the banks, bankers start regarding the previously accepted risk premiums to be excessive. The overall decline in risk premiums leads to growth in investment and growth in the price level of assets. To fund the increased level of investment and more speculative purchase of assets in a rising asset market, a greater number of external flows also contribute to the dynamics with the increased optimism of investors. This marks the start of "the euphoric economy" (Minsky, 1982).

Keen points out that in this state of the economy, both lenders and borrowers are confident about the future of the economy. During this period of rising asset prices, speculative demand for these assets increases further with expectations of

---

15 The ratio of credit to the financial sector to GDP rose to over 200 % prior to the crisis in 2007.

making more capital gains in the future. This also contributes to the increase in the asset prices in the market (real estate, financial assets). The liquidity of firms in the real sector is reduced by the rise in the debt to equity ratios, making firms more vulnerable to hikes in interest rates. However, increases in interest rates may not stop the boom, as expected yields from speculative investments may exceed the interest rates. This causes the demand for credit to grow more inelastic to changes in the interest rates.

This phase of Minsky"s "euphoric economy" also triggers another type of investor: "Ponzi financiers" (Minsky, 1982; Galbraith, 1955). These financiers make profits by trading during rising markets and acquire significant debt during the process. The cash flows from the business of these financiers may not be sufficient to cover the cost of serving the debts that they have acquired during the process. However, the euphorically expected future capital gains exceed these costs. Their role in this process not only causes further hikes in the interest rates but also contributes to the fragility of the system (Keen, 2013).

The dynamics of rising interest rates and increasing debt to equity ratios have a negative impact on the feasibility of many investment projects in the real sector of the economy. This leads many businesses and Ponzi investors to sell their assets, and these sales of assets cause breaks in the exponential growth of asset prices. Ponzi financiers with low cash flows to service their debt find themselves with assets that they can trade at a profit as well. This also causes banks to further increase the interest rates and curtail their lending as they realize that their customers are having difficulty in in paying their debts. This further contributes to the shortage of liquidity in the market, forcing holders of illiquid assets to sell them in return for liquidity. The dynamics of these events turns the euphoria into panic.

Keen (2013) also develops a generic model based on a system of differential equations that incorporate the essential features of Minsky's hypothesis, as pointed out earlier. The basic structure of the model is based on the Goodwin model for dynamic evolution of wages and employment. Although the model could be enriched to be more realistic, nevertheless, in its current form it does explain the dynamics of the Great Recession and the Great Moderation that preceded it. The results based on the simulations of the model are shown in Figures 3.3a and 3.3b.

Figure 3.3a Unemployment and Inflation in the USA

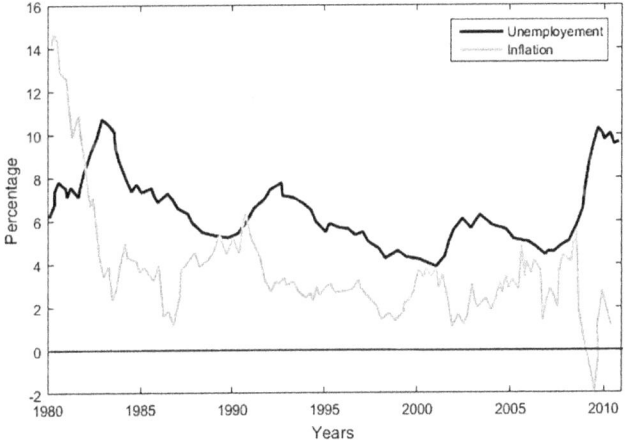

Source: Keen (2014)

Figure 3.3b Simulations based on Goodwin's Model

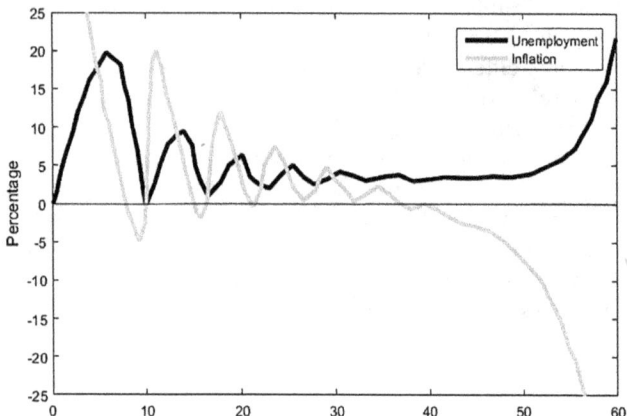

Source: Keen (2014)

In one of the recent financial stability reviews ECB (2015), reports that the growing trends in shadow banking sector, increase in the prices of financial assets and the rising sensitivity of these prices to market sentiments have significantly accounted for the potential financial fragility of the system. Financial innovations have, through the process of securitization, led to growth in speculative lending, while the financial markets have failed to provide sufficient credit to the real economy (Stockhammer, 2004 and Werner, 2012). Despite these developments in the financial sector, most macroeconomic models have failed to explain these phenomena. Furthermore, there has been no serious attempt to incorporate the relations between the financial sector and the real economy to explain the financial cycles endogenously.

Bezemer (2011) employs a simple balance sheet approach to highlight the important role played by the non-bank financial sector in contributing to the process of securitization and excessive lending by banks for speculative purposes. We present here his arguments in explaining financial fragility where he applies the important feature of stock-flow consistent (SFC) models that treats all transactions in the economy as credit/debit operations in balance sheets that should be equal in aggregate. This feature of equality of total credit and debit operations holds not only for a private firm, household or public sector, but it has to hold for the overall macro economy as well. The endogenous view of money that has been presented in this chapter, where banks have the ability to create new deposits has an important macroeconomic implication: money is credit. Therefore, its counterpart which is debt, should also be tracked to help our understanding of its dynamics and how it may induce financial instability. Bezemer, in these lines, defined the following simple balance sheet for the economy[16]:

$$L+S = D+W \qquad [7]$$

Here, L, S, D, W denote bank loans to the non-financial sector, securities assets held by the nonbank financial sector, deposits of the real sector (primarily used in the transactions of the real economy) and wealth of the real sector, respectively. In this simplified version of balance sheet, wealth (W) represents all the non-deposit assets held by the non-financial sector (this includes, housing, plant and machinery). This wealth is financed by the financial sector. All other non-deposit assets are excluded from this balance sheet as they

---

16 The left hand and right hand sides of the balance sheet represent assets and liabilities from the perspective of the financial sector. The mirror image of the same, therefore, represents the balance sheet of the non-financial sectors (households, firms and government).

cancel out against each other. For example, common stocks issued by firms or public debt issued by the government are implicit in W, without the specification of their distribution. Stocks held as assets by households are liabilities of the firms so they will cancel out with each other. Similarly, debt from nonfinancial firms to households is not indicated in the aggregated balance sheet.

In the process of credit extension, banks create deposits that are liabilities to themselves, and these credit flows help drive the real-sector and wealth transactions in the economy. The identity in [7], therefore, implies that whenever the economy's assets increase (D and W) its liabilities also increase. The newly created liquidity (L) by banks is used in the transactions of goods and services or in wealth transactions: $dL = dD + dW$. These new loans are liabilities of the real sector, inducing reverse flows of interest and principle repayments in future. In the SMM, these interest payments are ignored, but they are key to our understanding of the finance-induced instability of the system. In practice, the interest payments are converted into new loans (L) or into securities (S). In both cases, these repayment flows are converted into claims held by non-bank-financial sector on the real sector of the economy.

The nonbank financial sector plays an important role here as it accelerates the process of lending and debt accumulation. Additional demand for bank liabilities is generated when nonbank financial sector buys loans from banks and issues its own liabilities such as mortgage derivatives. These derivatives are tradable in the market and they become part of the total stock of financial assets. In short, nonbank financial sector can expand investment opportunities beyond real-sector investments, fueling the asset prices and growth in bank lending.

In the SMM, growth in D is the only monetary variable with any significance. The financial sector is not included explicitly; thus, S and W do not matter in SMM. Money in these models is simply a unit of account. Any growth in the real sector transactions is accommodated by growth of money. These assumptions in effect imply that

$$dS = dW = 0 \text{ and } dD = dY \qquad [8]$$

where Y is the nominal value of goods and services produced so that all money in the form of deposits is effectively assumed to be used in transactions of the real sector only.

The quantity theory of credit, presented in Chapter 3, showed that credit created for the real sector are in proportion to the size of economy measured as GDP and therefore $dD = dY$ indeed holds empirically. But there is an important caveat. Credit flows to the financial sector, issued by banks, have risen significantly in recent decades. This significant amount of debt is not taken into account by the SMM.

In the accounting sense, these flows to the financial sector are equal to the total lending minus growth in deposit money (dL+dS-dD), which is the excess of debt to the size of the economy which also contributes to the change in the wealth across the economy. This is what contributes to the economy-wide leverage, the debt-to-GDP ratio (L+S-D)/Y.

The fact that wealth cannot grow without growth in debt is based on the aggregate accounting identity and it is not an assumption. During the course of the credit boom, successive owners of assets may sell their assets with capital gain but the buyers will have to take the burden of more debt or withdraw liquidity from real-sector. At the micro level, trading in assets can be profitable to individuals but at macro level it has to be a 'zero sum' game.

During the boom-cycle in the asset markets, rising asset prices further induce demand for these assets in anticipation of continuing capital gains. The rise in asset prices also pushes the nominal value of the collateral that can be offered to borrow more money from the banks. That establishes a loop in which more lending to the financial sector leads to further hikes in asset prices that further boost the value of collateral and more credit to the financial sector. The US (prior to the global financial crises) and Japanese (prior to the collapse in the 1990s) experiences have clearly demonstrated this in practice.

This cycle can sustain itself for an extended period of time. However, as explained above, the ensuing increase in the economy-wide leverage. From the accounting perspective, the increase in debt is a liability of the real sector. Thus the real sector cash flows (or the financial assets whose prices are increasing but cash yields from them are not) have to take the burden of servicing the growing debt. The bubble collapses when flows from the real sector are not sufficient to service the debts and investors are forced to sell their assets in the market, causing an ultimate bust of the asset price bubble.

3.4. Balance Sheet Recession: An Explanation of Protracted Downturn

Koo (2011), among others, warns that the Western economies might be heading towards a Japan-like lost decade. He presents remarkable similarities between recent movements in housing prices in the Western economies and those in Japan 15 years ago (Figure 3.4). He argues that the post 2007–08 recession is not an ordinary recession; instead he draws a distinction between a normal recession and one driven by the deleveraging process of the post-crisis by the private sector. He contends that after the sudden and significant collapse of asset prices, the net worth of the private sector also encountered a huge drop. In order to restore financial health, the private sector (households and firms) are being forced to repair their balance sheets by increasing savings and repaying their debt. This process of deleveraging took the economy into deep recession as aggregate demand started falling.

As we had argued earlier, under the endogenous view of money, it is the creation of bank credit that injects liquidity into the system. As the private sector begins saving and paying down their debt in aggregate, it can lead to a decrease in the money supply, regardless of how much of base money is supplied by the central bank. The money supply (which is defined mostly as bank deposits) starts contracting as the private sector collectively draws down on these deposits by repaying debt. In the extreme case, when nobody borrows money from the banks, the money multiplier hits zero or even a negative value at margin.

Figure 3.4 Comparison of US housing prices with Japanese experience

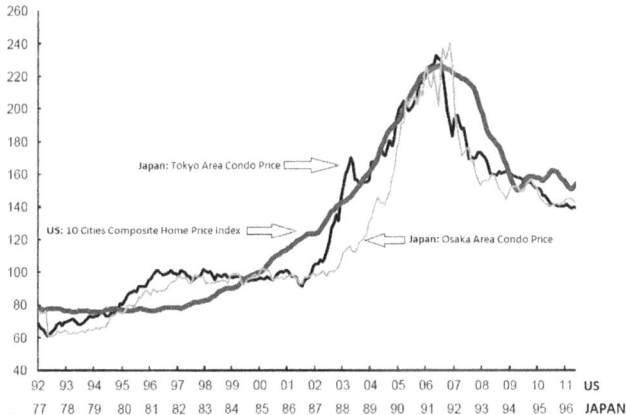

Source: Koo (2011)

In the absence of the endogenous view of money and with the exclusion of financial markets in the SMM approach, such behaviour may not be anticipated or visualized and may lead to prescribing policies that are not helpful in dealing with the situation.

The traditional prescriptions of monetary policy—reducing interest rates, as well as certain unusual measures like quantitative easing by the Federal Reserve, have not been effective in increasing aggregate demand. Massive injections of liquidity by the Federal Reserve in the US and Bank of England in the UK not only failed but had hardly any impact on the money supply (Figure 4.2).

Koo (2016) further explains that mainstream economics assumes that the private sector is forward-looking and therefore there will always be someone who will be willing to borrow money to invest when real interest rates are low enough. Until 2008, the private sector borrowers in the US and Europe responded to changes in interest rates. However, when the debt-financed bubble collapsed, the debt remained on the balance sheets while asset prices plunged. It required businesses and households to focus on paying down their debt despite the significant drop in the interest rates.

*Figure 3.5a Failure of liquidity injection to increase money supply
        (US)*

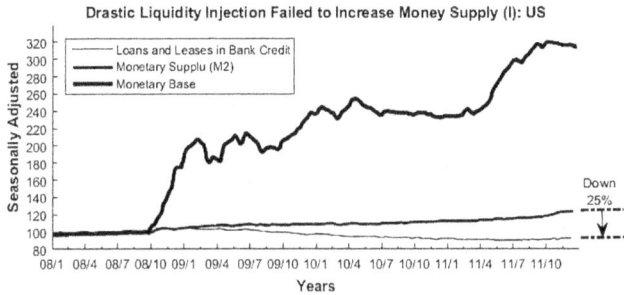

Drastic Liquidity Injection Failed to Increase Money Supply (I): US

Source: Koo (2011)

*Figure 3.5b Failure of liquidity injection to increase money supply
        (UK)*

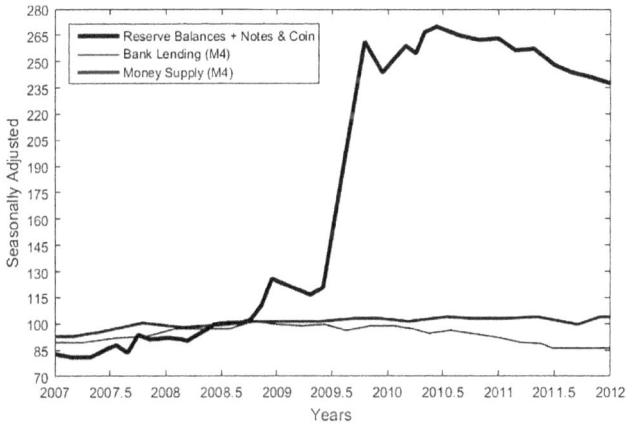

Source: Koo (2011)

One of the implications that Koo draws from this analysis is that, under these conditions, instead of subscribing to fiscal consolidation, fiscal stimulus is needed until the private sector has finished de-leveraging and is ready to borrow and spend savings.

Chapter IV
Two Different Faces of Money Creation[17]

Chapter 3 outlines three views of money creation process by banks: intermediation of loanable funds (ILF), fractional reserve banking (FRB) and financing through money creation (FMC). ILF generally forms the basis of theoretical models, where banks are mere intermediaries, just a neutral channel between savers and borrowers, one that cannot create any new credit money individually or collectively. In the FRB, although banks are still portrayed as financial intermediaries, money stock can only be expanded by the banking sector as a whole; no individual bank can create "money out of nothing." The FMC view, on the other hand, considers that individual banks create new credit money endogenously.

In this chapter the Accounting System Dynamics (ASD) modeling approach, developed by Yamaguchi (2013), is employed to explain the process of money creation by banks under the FRB and FMC theories.[18] It is shown that the two theories, FRB and FMC, have similar implications for banks creating money. The process whereby banks create this money can be dubbed the "debt-money" system. That is, money creation is linked to the creation of credit by banks[19].

---

17 This chapter is based on Yamaguchi and Yamaguchi (2016).

18 The FMC view incorporated here is a special case of the view presented earlier in Chapter 3. Simulation results reported in this chapter allow endogenous creation of money under FMC after an initial deposit of money. In practice, banks may not be constrained by deposits and/or reserves in creating money endogenously (Jakab et al., 2015; Fullwiler, 2013)

19 A detailed comparison of these two theories, using the ASD approach, is presented in the Appendix to this chapter.

Accounting System Dynamics (ASD) combines the principles of the System Dynamics (SD) approach with double entry accounting principles. SD approach employed here is based on computer simulation modeling technique to analyze complex nonlinear feedback systems and help in the design of policies to improve system performance. The macroeconomic model takes a holistic view of the economy, considering five sectors of the economy, such as central bank, commercial banks, consumers, firms and government. Yamaguchi (2013) has successfully developed ASD macroeconomics models allowing the integration of monetary and real sectors of the economy.[20]

In this chapter, we start with a review of the economic literature dealing with the concept of money and its functions. Next, based on the results of ASD model, we demonstrate that this debt-money system is unstable and point out a system design failure. Finally, we discuss the financial bubbles and bursts in Japan from this angle; the failure of the QE policies relates to the same system design problems.

4.1 Base Money as Legal Tender

The root cause of the failures of the SMM (whether neoclassical, Keynesian or monetarist) discussed in the previous chapters lies in the failure to properly incorporate role of financial sector and money in these models.

What is money, then? Where does it come from? These are fundamental questions that have been repeatedly raised through human history. Zarlenga (2002) quotes Aristotle's (384–322 BC) articulation on money as follows:

---

20 See Chapter 3 of Yamaguchi (2013) for more details about ASD modeling. SD modeling is also explained in detail in Yamaguchi (2013) Chapter 1 (*Money and Macroeconomic Dynamics*).

"It has the name *nomisma* – because *it exists not by nature, but by law (nomos)* and it is in our power to change it and make it useless." (Zarlenga, 2012: 34; emphasis added by the authors)

Following Aristotle, it is plausible to define money as *legal tender,* which is money that people cannot refuse to accept in exchange for a commodity. In other words, money is *legal tender* that co-flows inseparably along with the commodity as illustrated in Figure 4.1.

Figure 4.1 Co-flows of Money and Commodity[21]

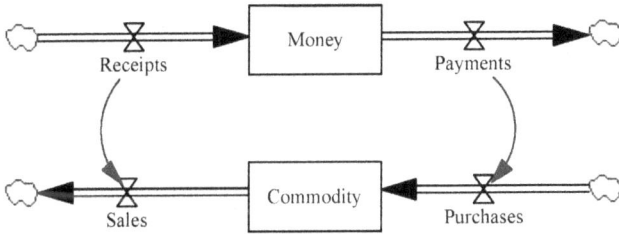

From the ASD modeling point of view, in order to model co-flows of money and commodity, at least the following three pieces of information on money are needed: money as stock, its unit to define the amount of stock, and the amount of its flow as a medium of exchange for goods and services. From these modeling requirements, three essential functions of money, as explained in many standard textbooks, can be derived:

21 The symbols used in these flow diagrams are as follows: Box represents Stock Variable, Arrows represent the flows, the Valves on the arrow is rate of flow and Cloud is the source of flow or sink of flow.

- Unit of Account (unit of money stock has to be determined before modeling);
- Medium of Exchange (flow amount of money stock has to be determined in relation to co-flow commodity);
- Store of Value (money has to be modeled as the amount of stock).

It is critical to emphasize that only when money is declared to be legal tender and put into circulation does it entail the three essential functions mentioned above, not *vice versa*.

Note, however, that Adam Smith contradicted Aristotle's definition of money, as follows:

> "By the money price of goods it is to be observed, I understand always, *the quantity of pure gold and silver* for which they are sold, without any regard to denomination of the coin." (Zerlanga, 2002: 313)

Advancing his idea more axiomatically, many textbooks currently define money as a commodity that meets the above three functions. According to this axiom of money, gold and silver are best qualified as ideal money *by nature*, because their physical nature meets the three functional conditions of money perfectly. This reversed definition of money has become a root cause of confusion for economists, as well as ordinary people, who are heavily influenced by them. According to the double-entry bookkeeping rule of accounting, commodity transactions with cash money in Figure 4.1 can be described in Table 4.1 as follows.

Table 4.1 Journal Entries of Transactions with Money

Buyers		Sellers	
Debit (Assets)	Credit (Assets)	Debit (Assets)	Credit (Assets)
Commodity (+)	Cash (-)	Cash (+)	Commodity (-)

In such transactions, buyers have to give up their cash assets to increase their commodity assets, while for sellers commodity assets have to be given up to increase their cash assets. In short, commodity transactions with cash are always booked as an increase and decrease of assets simultaneously.

Issuance of Legal Tender

In order to define money as legal tender, there must be specific laws that stipulate the legal issuance of money. In Japan, for example, the Currency Unit and Money Issuance Act (revised in 1987) and the Bank of Japan Act (revised in 1997) enable the Bank of Japan to issue coins and banknotes. Consequently, in Japan, *currency*, consisting of government *coins* and Bank of Japan *notes*, is specifically defined by law as legal tender, such that it cannot be refused as a means of payment; that is why an alternative name for it is *fiat money*. Figure 4.2 illustrates the state of currency (coins and notes) as legal tender.

Once currency is put into circulation as legal tender under the FRB system, it begins split into two parts: currency outstanding and reserves with the central bank. The sum of these parts is called *base money*. Hence, base money is by definition legal tender (Figure 4.2):

$$Base\ Money = Currency\ Outstanding + Reserves \qquad [1]$$

Figure 4.2 Base Money as Legal Tender

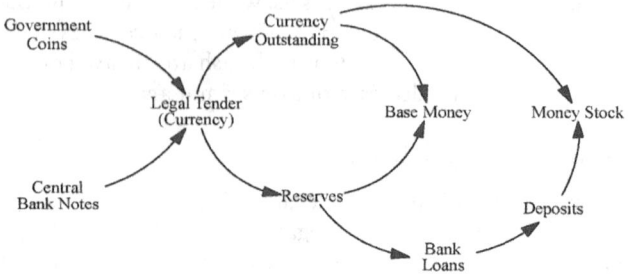

Figure 4.3 Issuance of Base Money Backed by Various Types of Assets

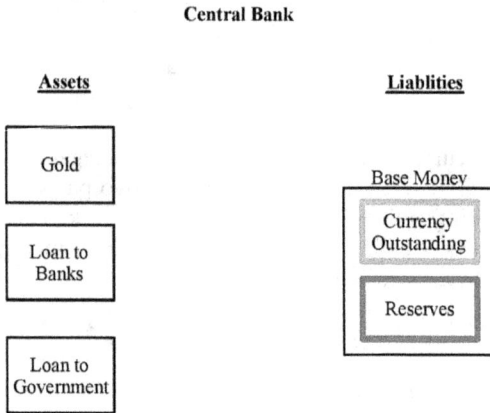

Although the central bank is legally allowed to issue base money, it can issue base money only when someone comes to borrow at interest. Those who come to borrow from the central bank are mainly commercial banks and government. Base money is issued through various lending facilities or asset purchases (Figure 4.3) using the double-entry accounting rule. Base money is booked as liabilities on the balance sheet of the central bank, and backed by various types of assets, such as gold, discount loans to commercial banks and loans to the government (securities).

4.1.1 Deposits as "Functional-Money Out of Nothing"

Under the debt money system, banks create deposits by granting loans, collectively, to the non-banking public sector. Deposits thus created are used for transactions as if they are money (Figure 4.4).

Figure 4.4 Deposits as Functional-Money

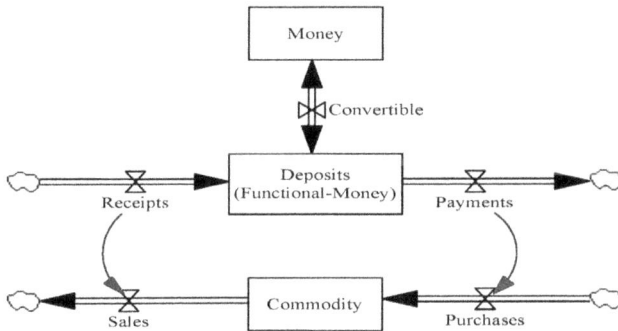

Table 4.2 Journal Entries of Transaction with Deposits

Buyers		Sellers	
Debit (Assets)	Credit (Assets)	Debit (Assets)	Credit (Assets)
Commodity (+)	Deposits (-)	Deposits (+)	Commodity (-)

Using double-entry accounting principle, this transaction is booked as in Table 4.2. Hence, all transactions are booked within the account of assets as in Table 4.1. Does this mean that deposits, created by banks, become legal tender, similar to cash, such that no one can refuse to accept? According to Masaaki Shirakawa, former governor of the Bank of Japan, the answer is negative.

> "Contrary to the central bank notes, creditors can refuse to accept bank deposits as the payments of debt obligations because of credit risks associated with bankruptcies of debtors' banks. However, in normal times, bank deposits *function as money* because of creditors' confidence that bank deposits can be converted to central bank notes." (Shirakawa, 2008: 13; emphasis added by the authors)

What is meant here is that deposits are accepted for commodity transactions in Figure 4.4 only when their convertibility to money is presumed by their recipients. In this sense, they are not legal tender. Henceforth, we may regard deposits as *functional-money,* technically different from legal tender. Based on the assumption that deposits function as money, standard textbooks define another concept of monetary aggregate in addition to *money* as

Money Stock = Currency in Circulation + Deposits   [2]

Money stock thus defined is the total amount of money available in the economy as a medium of exchange for the regulation of transactions and economic activities.

On the other hand, though this concept of money stock is theoretically rigorous in capturing the amount of money available in the economy, it is hard to calculate it statistically in practice. Accordingly, money stock is obtained more practically according to the monetary data available at the central bank and commercial banks using the following formula:

Money Stock (Data) = Currency Outstanding + Deposits   [3]

This relation is illustrated in Figure 4.2. The difference in these two definitions is the "vault cash" held by commercial banks such that:

Currency Outstanding = Currency in Circulation + Vault cash (Banks) [4]

Money stock defined in (4) begins to play a role as money as it is legal tender under the assumption of its convertibility with money.

4.2 System Design Failures of Debt Money: Instability of the Functional-Money Stock

With the analysis in the foregoing section, it has been shown that the current monetary system is unstable in the sense that it causes booms and busts and has led to recent failures of QE policy. In other words, the debt money system demonstrably entails system design failures.

4.2.1 Liquidity Preference in the Non-Banking Sector

The current debt money system that creates functional-money could be a good system because money necessary for our economic activities it can create this money at no cost! However, to the contrary, it turns out to be a faulty system, as will be discussed from now on, in the sense that it causes monetary and financial instabilities, followed by booms and busts, economic recessions, unemployment, income inequalities, and other issues.

Without losing generality, our analysis from this point utilizes the FMC approach of functional-money creation[22]. There are several factors under the debt-money system that cause monetary instabilities in the current system. The first factor we investigate here is fluctuations of the currency ratio (α), which is the ratio of currency in circulation to total deposits.

Though cash is becoming used less and less as a means of transaction, thanks to information technology (particularly in Nordic countries such as Sweden and Finland), bank notes and government coins still comprise an indispensable means for payments in relatively smaller transactions. In Japan, for example, not only a relatively higher currency ratio is observed (about 15 percent of money stock M1), but a cyclical demand for bank notes from season to season is reported by the Bank of Japan (Bank of Japan, 2011). Accordingly, meeting depositors' demands for such cash withdrawal, banks have to make sure that they have sufficient reserves to meet this demand and to avoid possible bank runs during economic recessions or depressions.

How does the fluctuation of the currency ratio affect money stock (data) then? Our simulation analysis in this section is carried out in the above case of discount loans of \$100 by the central bank to commercial banks[23]. And the public sector (producers, consumers and non-banking financial institutions) is assumed to react the business cycle

---

22 In the ASD model, FMC theory of money creation has been interpreted as Stock Approach (Appendix to Chapter 4).

23 A Juglar business cycle of 8 years has been created by since function, and normal distribution with mean =0 and standard deviation=0.2.

by changing their attitudes toward liquidity preferences (that is, currency ratios).

Figure 4.5 Currency Ratio Fluctuations and Money Stock Instability

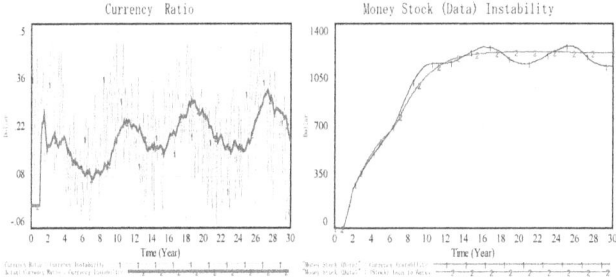

Coarse fluctuations of the currency ratio caused by these random behaviors are illustrated in the left-hand diagram of Figure 4.5 (line 1). Yet behaviors of the actual currency ratio (= Currency in Circulation / Deposits (Banks)) are smoothed out over the soft business cycle of eight years (line 2). The right hand diagram shows how these fluctuations of currency ratios cause instability in money stock (line 1) compared with the stable money stock (line 2), when the currency ratio is held constant at $\alpha = 0.2$. Figure 4.6 is enlarged with additional behaviours. Base money (line 1) in the figure is kept stable, though currency in circulation (line 3) fluctuates cyclically. This stable base money vividly contrasts with the cyclical fluctuations of money stock (line 2) and bank loans (line 5).

The main conclusion of the simulation exercise is evident. Under the debt money system, even stable base money (stable monetary policy) creates unstable money stock.

Figure 4.6 Stable Base Money and Money Stock Instability

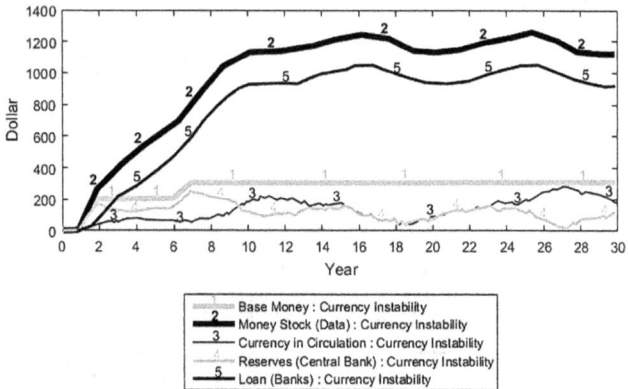

4.2.2 Lending Behavior of Commercial Banks

Instability of money stock is also caused by the lending behavior of banks. In addition to the same economic case of a
discount loan of $100, as above, let us further assume that
bankers are impatient and want to make more loans out of
their maximum loanable fund for a shorter lending period.
Specifically, we assume that bankers make loans of 60 percent of loanable funds (instead of 30 percent) over one year
(instead of over 3 years); that is, Lending Ratio = 0.6 and
Lending Time = 1 in the model here.

Figure 4.7 Impatient Lending Behavior Overshoot the Money Stock

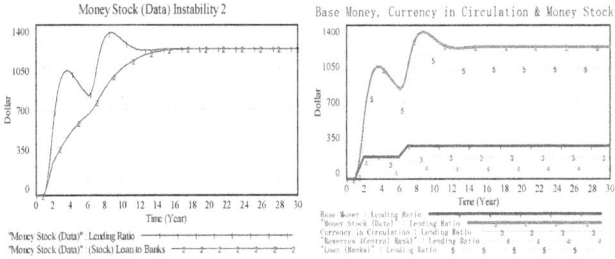

The results are presented in Figure 4.7. The left-hand panel illustrates the overshoot and the fluctuation of money stock (line 1) compared with the stable case (line 2). The right hand panel indicates that this overshoot behavior of money stock (line 2) occurs even under the stable base money (line 1) and stable currency in circulation (line 3). The current debt money system allows banks to earn additional interest income through creation of the functional deposits compared to ILF approach and it widens the scope of short-termism according to their business model. The model encourages short-termism because it makes long-term investments relatively more expensive (Lietaer, 2012) The results and conclusions presented here are similar to the previous section: unstable money stock is caused by short-termism of bankers.

4.2.3 Destruction of Functional-Money by Debt Repayments (Simulation Based)

So far we have focused on the creation of functional-money and money stock. Inversely, the same debt money system can destroy money stock instantaneously whenever debts are repaid. In section 3.4 of Chapter 4, we had presented one of the explanations of protracted downturn in economic activities due to balance sheet recession after the financial crisis (Koo (2011). The total money stock can deplete significantly due to deleveraging process of the private sector after the crisis.

In the simulation presented above, where, in addition to the discount loan of $100 as above, let us further assume that the private sector (mainly producers or corporations) continues to repay 20 percent of their debts, that is, a repayment ratio=0.2, for two decades, starting at the year t=10. This assumption corresponds to the economic case in Japan, where, after the burst of the bubble around the mid-1990s, many Japanese corporations were forced to repay their debts to escape the underwater situation of their net assets caused by the massive depreciation of their financial assets in order to restore their balance sheet. Japan has been suffering from this balance sheet recession for almost two decades.

Figure 4.8 presents the results, showing how bank loans (line 5) and money stock (line 2) can be incessantly and concurrently destroyed by repayments. Base money (line 1) as well as currency in circulation (line 3) stays stable, yet money stock is decimated. Whenever money stock drops precipitously, it can have severe macroeconomic implications. It can lead to deep recession with low economic activity and high unemployment rates.

Figure 4.8 Destruction of Functional-Money by Debt Repayments

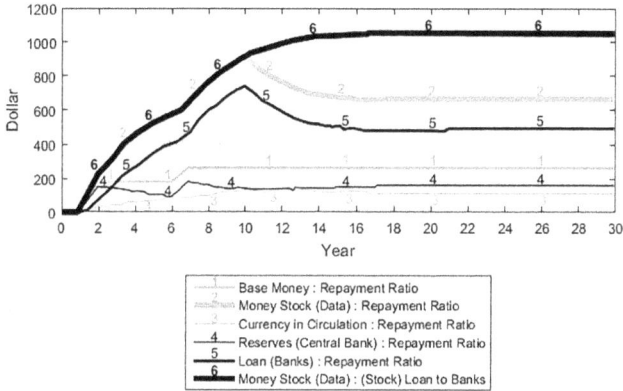

This massive destruction of functional-money in the simulation results here were also verified, during the Great Depression between 1929 and 1933 in the USA. Irving Fisher (1935: 6–7) described the phenomenon more metaphorically as follows.

> "This loss, or destruction, of 8 billion of check-book money[24] has been realized by few and seldom mentioned. There would have been big newspaper headlines if 8 thousand miles out of 23 thousand miles of railway had been destroyed. Yet such a disaster would have been a small one compared with the destruction of 8 billion out of 23 billion of our main monetary highway. That destruction of 8 billion dollars of what the public counted on as their money was the chief sinister fact in the depression from which followed the two chief tragedies, unemployment and bankruptcies."

---

24 That is, the loss of demand deposits between 1929 and 1933 (Fisher; 1935: 6–7).

4.3 Financial Bubbles and Bursts in Japan

Another historical case of the destruction of bank loans happened in Japan after the burst of her asset price bubbles around the mid-1990s. Japanese bubbles were mainly fueled by functional-money creation by commercial banks to the non-bank financial sector,[25] which further on-lent those funds to business enterprises (including SMEs) at higher interest rates.

As in the Great Depression in 1929, the asset bubbles in the Japanese economy could not hold their breath for a long time. Prices of financial and real assets (stocks, real estate) hit their peak in the mid-1990s, followed by the collapses. As Figure 4.9 demonstrates, total bank loans (line 5) in balance sheets had skyrocketed until the mid-1990s. Then, numerous companies who had borrowed a massive amount of functional-money were faced with insolvency. Accordingly, they were forced to repay their debts, reducing their loans as illustrated by line 3. This caused prolonged economic recession and stagnation for two decades and the Japanese GDP remained stagnant (line 5).

Yet, contrary to our explanation so far and to the historical facts during the Great Depression, Japanese M1 and M3 (lines 6 and 2) continued to grow irrespective of the loss of loans. That is, the destruction of bank loans was not followed by the destruction of money stocks.

---

25 Nonbanks are private institutions that raise funds by methods other than deposits and deposit-like instruments. They invest funds through loans with interest rates usually higher than that of bank loans. Nonbanks in Japan include finance companies and structured- financing special purpose companies (SPCs) and trusts.

This happened because of two reasons. First, the effect of destruction of bank loans were counter-balanced by the massive government deficit followed by the QE policies in the form of exceptional open market purchases by the Bank of Japan from March 2001 through March 2006. Second, QE restarted in 2013 as indicated by the increases in base money M0 (line 1).

Figure 4.9 Bubbles-Bursts followed by QE Policies in Japan

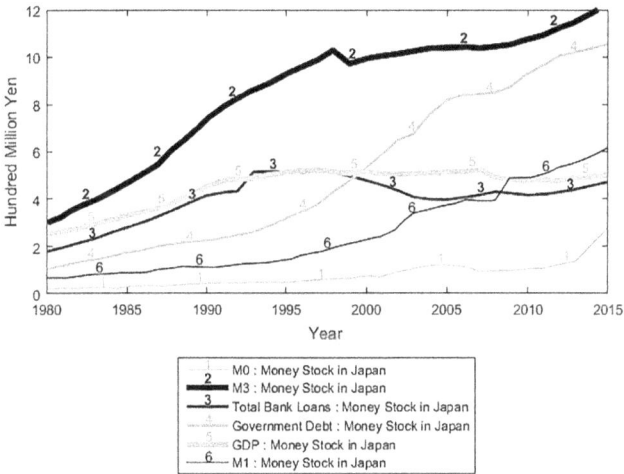

Figure 4.9 Bubbles-Bursts followed by QE Policies in Japan

4.3.1 Impediments to QE Policies

To understand this anomaly in Japan, discussed in the previous subsection, let us investigate the expected impact of QE policies on the money stock. QE policies introduced after the global financial crisis in Japan, the US and the EU aimed at increasing the money stock through massive purchases of mainly government securities. That would directly increase the base money with the hope that the increased money stock would eventually stimulate economic activities and thus GDP growth.

Figure 4.10 Debt Repayment

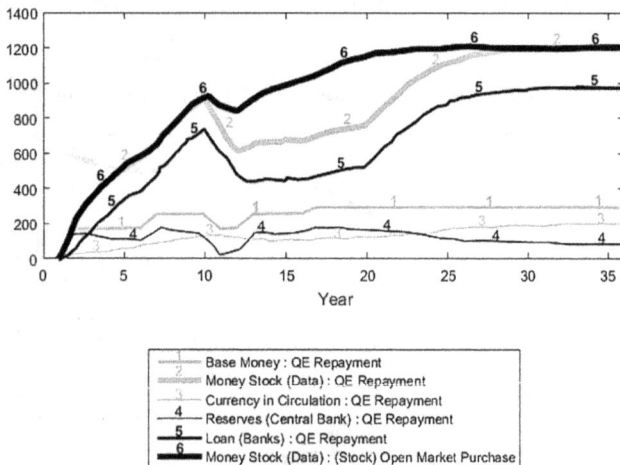

Yet, in reality all the ongoing QE policies seem to have failed due to the massive destruction of bank loans and the balance sheet recession as discussed above. Simulation results for an open market operation of 50 percent at t=16 increases base money (line 1) in the following year (Figure 4.10) illustrate this phenomenon. Since bank loans (line 5) are destroyed due to the repayments, money stock (line 2) is also destroyed. Under the circumstances, the increase in base money fails to increase the money stock to the level where repayments do not exist (line 6). Worse, the monetary authority and the government have no direct control over this failure. Apparently, it is caused by the monetary instabilities built into the current debt money system.

In the simulations, it is assumed that after a decade-long balance sheet recession, the non-banking public sector has completed its repayments and the money stock (line 2) begins to increase to the previous level (line 6). What will happen if, under this recovery, the currency ratio begins to fluctuate again?

Figure 4.11 Failures of QE Caused by Repayments and Liquidity Fluctuations

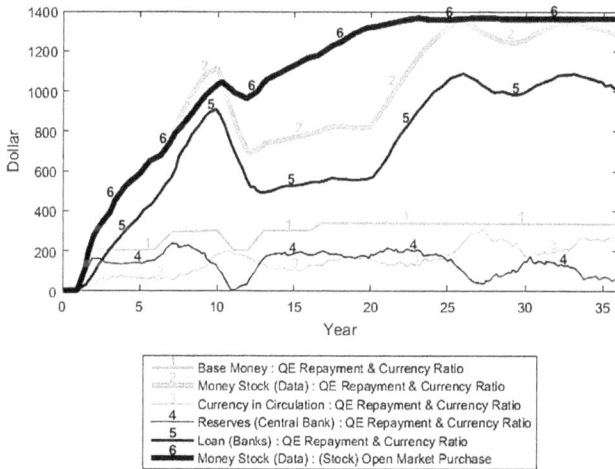

```
                Base Money : QE Repayment & Currency Ratio
        2 ----- Money Stock (Data) : QE Repayment & Currency Ratio
                Currency in Circulation : QE Repayment & Currency Ratio
        4 ----- Reserves (Central Bank) : QE Repayment & Currency Ratio
        5       Loan (Banks) : QE Repayment & Currency Ratio
        6       Money Stock (Data) : (Stock) Open Market Purchase
```

Figure 4.11 shows that this recovery is again hindered by the fluctuation of the currency ratio or liquidity preferences; the money stock (line 2) becomes cyclical and unstable. Worse, the fluctuation of liquidity preferences cannot be under direct control of either the central bank or the government. In other words, QE policy is destined to face structural obstruction under the current debt money system and economic conditions behind it. Thus this approach explains the ineffectiveness of the QE policies in Japan.

4.3.2 Failures of QE Policies in Japan

To investigate the actual behavior of monetary aggregates in Japan by QE policies in relation to the base money, let us examine how M1 and M3 have been affected by the changes in M0. For this purpose, behaviors in Figure 4.9 are normalized so that all data values become 100 in the year 2000 in Figure 4.12.

As explained above, QE policy is nothing but the exceptional open market purchases of government securities and other commercial bonds held by banks to increase base money, or more specifically bank reserves. The Bank of Japan introduced QE policy in March, 2001, through March, 2006, as the first trial policy among major economies. As a result, during this period base money M0 (line 1) increased, which also seemed to have increased demand deposits M1 (line 6) simultaneously, despite the massive destruction of bank loans (line 5). However, as pointed out by Koo (2011), this increase in M1 was actually caused by the massive injection of government debt (line 2), counter-balancing the destruction of bank loans.

Following the Second Great Depression, the so-called Lehman Shock in 2008, the Bank of Japan was forced to reintroduce the QE policy for the second time in April of 2013, increasing its base money (reserves) by 131.3 trillion yen through April 2015[26]. Accordingly, the base money has

---

26 Figures used in the argument here are based on Yamaguchi and Yamaguchi (2015).

increased by 150.8 trillion yen during last two years from 149.5 trillion yen to 300.3 trillion yen, an increase of almost fourfold since 2000 (line 1). Yet money stock M1 only increased this time by 57.2 trillion yen, from 560.9 trillion yen to 618.1 trillion yen. The money multiplier, which is a ratio between money stock and base money, was 3.75 in 2013. If it had stayed stable, as most QE policy makers had expected, the increase in base money by 150.8 trillion yen could have increased money stock by the amount of 565.5 trillion yen! Yet, it only increased by 57.2 trillion yen, about ten percent of the expected amount. If this increase in base money were to be done as helicopter money, it would have increased money stock by at least the same amount of 150.8 trillion yen. Traditional macroeconomic theory has completely failed to explain this failure of QE policies in Japan.

Figure 4.12 Failures of QE policy in Japan

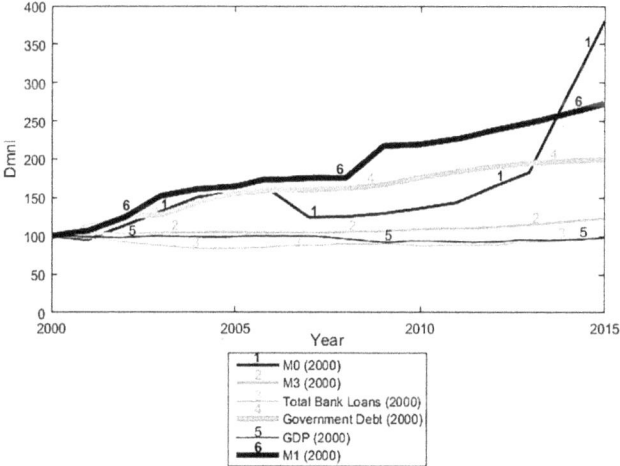

91

Concurrently, QE policies have been heavily applied to the depressed economies of the US and EU countries as their last resort of financial policy to stimulate their economies. Unfortunately, they have also failed, as in Japan. The failures of QE policies as "last resort" imply the failure of system design of the current debt money system of banking. As an unprecedented last resort, the Bank of Japan was further pushed to introduce its "negative interest rate policy (NIRP)" on January 29, 2016! For system dynamics researchers, it seems to be an ineffectual struggle that further exacerbates a system design failure.

4.4 System Design Failures of Debt Money: A Summary

4.4.1 Business Model of Banks

The current debt money system of has been shown here to have built-in system design failures, in the sense that it causes monetary instabilities leading to booms and busts, economic recessions, and unemployment, etc. Even recent QE policies that had been expected to save our sinking economies as a last resort have also failed.

What is the driving force, then, causing these system design failures in the current debt money system? It is the incessant motivation of bankers for higher interest revenues as their profits. The business model for bankers is to make loans as large as possible and collect interest revenues from these loans. In a market-based economy, banks do formulate strategy based on their "business model" as corporate businesses do to maximize profits[27].

---

27 The optimal strategy in the "business model of commercial banks," interest income, encourages short-termism because

The problem lies in banking system itself, which drives the business activities of banks into wild bubbles. Once bubbles get started, investors can profit through capital gains, but these gains are not accounted for in GDP and contribute to a rising debt to GDP ratio. It is the real sector of the economy that has to take the burden of servicing the excessive debt generated in the process, which in the end becomes the cause of crises. This constitutes a positive feedback loop of bubbles. In other words, the banking system has a built-in positive feedback loop that contributes to driving bubbles as illustrated in Figure 4.13. the implications of this positive feedback loop had also been dealt in detail in chapter 3 of this book.

Bubbles inevitably have to burst. With their inability to sustain the growing burden of debt, investors are forced to sell their assets, which causes the assets market to crumble (Chapter 3) Positive-sum games from the perspective of speculators now turn into horrifying *negative-sum games* in which all investors lose, and public losses continue to accumulate as illustrated in Figure 4.13. Under the circumstance, corporations are forced to repay their debt, which in turn destroys money stock as discussed above, and shrinks economic activities due to the shortage of liquidity or money stock, as explained by Koo (2011), in terms of a "balance sheet recession." That is, a balancing feedback loop begins to dominate the positive feedback loop.

---

long-term investments relative to the short-term are more expensive (Lietaer et al. 2012). The latest Basel III capital requirements are aimed at reducing the risk of default by banks; however, deregulations have also allowed banks to circumvent these conditions by moving various liabilities off their balance sheets (Fullwiler, 2013).

*Figure 4.13 Driving Force of Instability: Unearned Interest
Revenues*

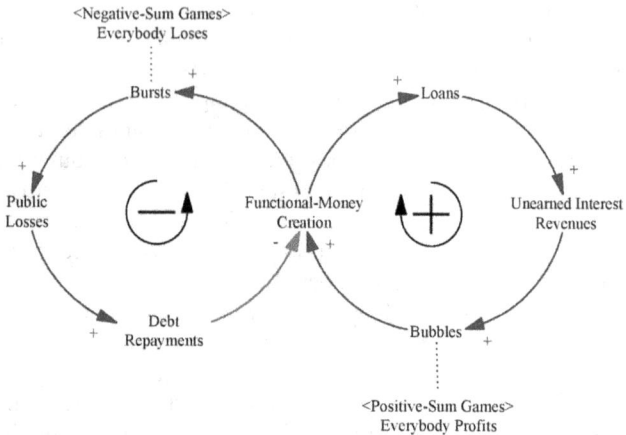

Yamaguchi (2013, Chapter 14) develops a comprehensive
ASD macroeconomic model, by integrating the real and financial sectors of the economy[28]. He provides detailed results
based on the simulations of the model under different scenarios. The reinforcing loop of credit creation and its balancing loop of credit crunch (4.13) in the model explains the
dynamics of income inequality under the debt money system.
It also shows how the system can generate destabilizing cycles
of recessions and inflation. On the other hand, the proposed
public money system is visibly more stable in these respects.

In conclusion, it is being demonstrated that the driving
forces of monetary instabilities is embedded in the current

---

28 Given the scope of this book, the details of the model specification are not discussed here.

debt money system, tied to bank loans under the so-called fractional reserve banking system. The credit flows to the financial sector do not contribute to GDP, but the interest payments are derived from the income generated in the real sector of the economy.

4.4.2 Can We Re-design a Failed System?

If airplane crashes occur repeatedly, engineers will try to figure out whether these are caused by human error or system design failures. When crashes are identified as the fault of system design errors, engineers will be forced to draw new designs for the planes. Thanks to their repeated efforts at re-design, we have now acquired the safest airplane system in human history.

In a similar fashion, monetary instabilities discussed so far have been identified as system design failures of fractional reserve banking. Faced with the ongoing financial crises and accumulating government debts triggered by the instability of the current debt money system, economists are now, like engineers of airplanes, obliged to re-design our failing monetary and economic system. Can they re-design it?

4.5 Conclusions

In this chapter, we attempted to demonstrate that the current debt money system of fractional reserve banking entails monetary instabilities; booms and busts are repeatedly triggered, followed by inflation-deflation cycles, recessions, unemployment, income inequalities, etc. Moreover, recent QE policies aiming at overcoming these instabilities are also shown to have failed. As an exemplifying case, the failure of the QE policies in Japan are explored in detail. With these observations in mind, the conclusion is that the current debt money system entails system design failures.

Appendix to Chapter IV

The processes of money creation by banks under FRB and FMC, using the ASD approach, are being discussed here. In following the norms of the ASD model, the FRB approach can be considered a "flow" approach, in which, through multiple series of transactions, the banking system as a whole can collectively expand money supply. On the other hand, the FMC approach can be interpreted as a "stock" approach, which presumes that a single bank can create money endogenously, out of nothing.

A.1. Flow Approach of Money Creation (FRB)

We follow the system dynamics approach of Yamaguchi (2013)[29] enhanced by the role of the central bank as the depository bank for the government without changing behaviors of the government, central bank and commercial banks. We assume that commercial banks run their primary business by accepting savings (deposits) from depositors and making loans to investors. Accordingly, banks are assumed to be intermediaries just like other financial institutions. Figure A.1 illustrates this banking practice as intermediaries. The itemized numbers below are the same as those in the figure.

1) First, banks collect deposits from the non-banking public sector consisting of households, producers and non-banking financial institutions in our model. Under the current fractional reserve banking system, a portion of deposits thus collected is required to be held with the cen-

---

29 Chapter 5 of the book.

tral bank to avoid risks of cash deficiencies according to a required reserve ratio (β) such that

$$\beta = Resrves / Deposits \tag{1}$$

2) The remaining deposits are loaned out to borrowers. Since the public as a whole does not need to hold the entire amount of cash at hand as liquidity, a portion of cash is deposited with banks according to its currency ratio(α) such that:

$$Currency\ Ratio = \alpha = Currency\ in\ Circulation / Deposits \tag{2}$$

Figure A.1: Flow Approach of Money Creation

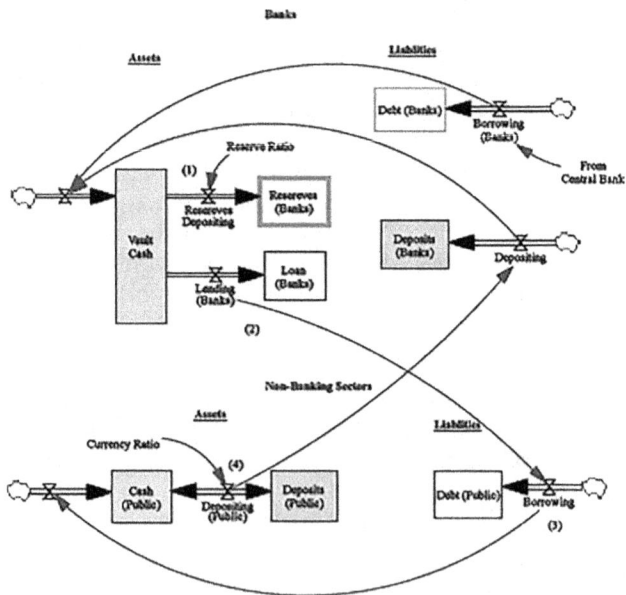

We derive and show the money multiplier m as a ratio between money stock and high-powered money. Then, the money multiplier can be calculated as follows.

$$m \frac{\text{Money stock}}{\text{High Powered Money}} = \frac{\text{Currency in Circulation} + \text{Deposits}}{\text{High PoweCurrency in Circulation} + \text{Reserves}} \quad [3]$$

This can be further manipulated to reach

$$m = \frac{\alpha+1}{\alpha+\beta} \quad [4]$$

Accordingly, money stock defined in equation [2] in chapter 3 can be alternatively calculated in terms of m (α and β) as follows:

*Money Stock = m * High – Powered Money*   [5]

In this way, by calculating the actual currency ratio and reserve ratio at each time step in our model as illustrated in Figure A.2, money stock can be dynamically obtained. Money stock thus calculated includes deposits as functional-money. To calculate the portion of legal tender out of the money stock in circulation, equation [3] in chapter 3 can be rewritten as

*High – Powered Money (as legal tender) = mc * Money Stock*   [6]

where *mc* is defined as the *money convertibility coefficient*. The coefficient thus defined is obviously a reciprocal of the money multiplier *mc=1/m*.

Under the default assumption of coefficient values in our model; that is, $\alpha = 0.2$ and $\beta=0.1$, the money multiplier becomes $m = 4$, and the money convertibility coefficient becomes $c = 0.25$[30]. That is to say, only 25 percent of the

---

30   When $\beta = 1$ (100 % reserve requirement) under the public money system discussed in Chapter 5, we have $m = mc = 1$ so that the entire amount of money stock in circulation becomes legal tender.

functional money stock can be convertible to *genuine money* as legal tender. This implies that under the fractional reserve banking in our model, for instance, only 25 percent of the money stock in circulation for transactions can be convertible to legal tender[31].

Figure A.2: *Money Stock Definitions*

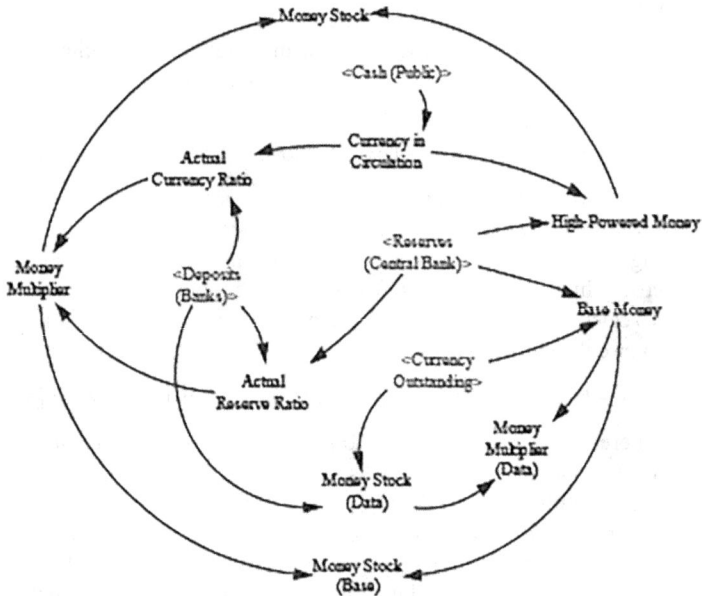

---

31 In the UK, the convertibility ratio is around 3 percent.

A.2 Double-Entry Accounting Presentation of the Flow Approach

Banks that act in practice as intermediaries are now described according to the double-entry bookkeeping rule. In the flow approach, bank loans do not seem to create deposits, simply because banks are assumed to make loans out of cash assets in the model as shown in top left balance sheet of Banks in Table A.1. In other words, banks increase their loan assets to gain interest revenues by giving up their own cash assets.

Table A.1: Journal Entries of the Flow Approach

Banks		Non-Banking Public Sector	
Debit (Assets)	Credit (Assets)	Debit (Assets)	Credit (Liabilities)
Loan (+)	Cash (-)	Cash (+)	Debt (+)

Debit (Assets)	Credit (Liabilities)	Debit (Assets)	Credit (Assets)
Cash (+)	Deposits (+)	Commodity (+)	Cash (-)

This transaction seems fair and reasonable as a profit-seeking strategy using their cash assets. Where does that cash come from, then? Surely it is tied to deposits as shown in the bottom left balance sheet of Banks. When cash accounts are canceled out in this balance sheet, bank loans (debit of assets) can be said to be balanced by deposits (credit of liabilities)[32]. In this situation can the banks, then, make loans out of these deposits at their disposal? The demand deposits are for trans-

---

32 Whenever transactions are traced back in this way, the balance sheet of the flow approach becomes structurally the same as that of the stock approach, as shown in Table A.1 below. In the flow approach, loans are made out of deposits (Deposits→Loan), while in the stock approach, deposits are made out of loans (Loan→Deposits).

actional purposes, and banks are obliged to hold them any-time to meet withdrawal requests from depositors. Yet, Irving Fisher once pointed out: "When money is deposited in a checking account (i.e. demand deposits), the depositor still thinks of the money as his, though *legally it is the bank's*" (Fisher, 1935: 1; emphasis by the authors). Hence, deposits are legally owned by the banks and they can make loans from their depositors' money[33].

Hence, in the flow approach the credit creation process out of nothing is not so apparent as the double-entry book-keeping practice gives the impression that banks are making loans out of cash. This may explain why the FRB approach is used by mainstream economists, as it still portrays banks as financial intermediaries. The deposits created in this process constitute a large portion of transactions in the economy that are not legal tender, as illustrated in Figure A.1.

A.3 Stock approach of money creation (FMC)

Let us now explore the stock approach to the lending practic-es of banks, illustrated by Figure A.3. The itemized numbers below are the same as those indicated in Figure A.1.

---

33 In Japan, this practice is guaranteed by Article 590, Civil Code.

Figure A.3. Stock Approach of Money Creation.

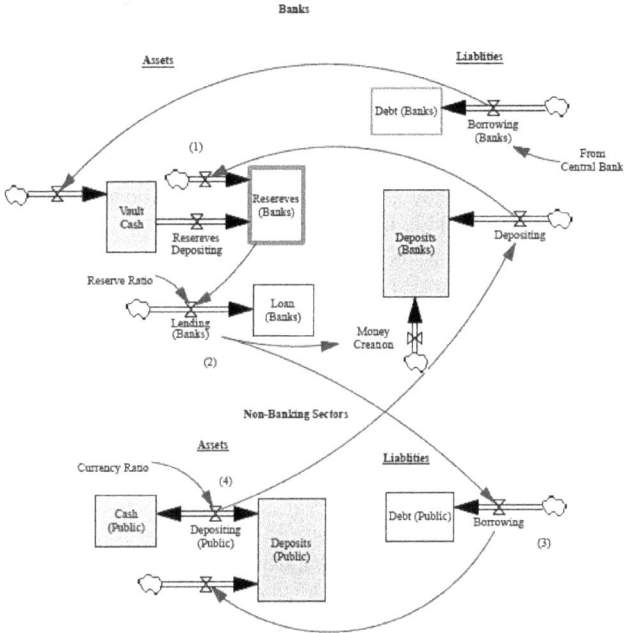

Table A.2: Transactions of Non-Banking Sectors: Flow Approach

Buyers		Sellers	
Debit (A)	Credit (A)	Debit (A)	Credit (A)
Commodity (+)	Cash (-)	Cash (+)	Commodity (-)
Commodity (+)	Deposits (-)	Deposits (+)	Commodity (-)

1) Whenever banks collect deposits, they can reserve the entire amount of deposits with the central bank[34].
2) In the fractional reserve banking system, maximum loanable funds are calculated according to the following formula[35]:

Maximum Loanable Funds= (Bank Reserves / Required Reserve Ratio) – Bank Deposits = $((1-\beta)/\beta)$ Bank Reserves [7]

Banks enter these loans as deposits with the borrowers' deposit accounts. This lending practice of loans differs from the flow approach, as the bank can create $((1-\beta)/\beta)$ factors of functional-money out of nothing in a single transaction. So, the stock approach demonstrates that banks can create credit endogenously as in FMC, but the maximum amount that they can create individually is constrained by the reserve requirement (β)[36].

---

34 In the stock approach model, deposits are assumed to go directly into "Reserves (Banks)." In practice, when customers put deposits at the bank, they are first debited as "Cash (Banks)" instead of "Reserves (Banks)" as in the flow approach. Deposits of cash in the stock approach are assumed to be directly debited as Reserves, and the amount of Vault Cash is later adjusted according to liquidity demand by the non-banking sector.

35 The last equation holds only when a bank's deposits are fully reserved with the central bank; that is Bank Deposits = Bank Reserves.

36 As noted earlier, this restraint on the maximum amount an individual bank can create after an initial injection of fiat money is not applicable in many advanced economies, where there is no reserve requirement. Furthermore, Fullwiler (2013) explains that under the "Corridor System" of banking, banks are not constrained by deposits and/or reserves in creating credit money.

A.4 Double-Entry Accounting Presentation of the Stock Approach

Banking practice using the stock approach according to the double-entry bookkeeping rule is presented in Table A.2.

The difference from the flow approach, as depicted in Tables A.1 and A.2, is evident. In the flow approach, bank loans (+) (debit assets) are increased at the cost of cash (-) (credit assets), while in the stock approach, they increase simultaneously with the deposits (+) (credit liabilities). In other words, in the flow approach the banks' assets are cancelled out, while in the stock approach, without sacrificing cash assets, banks can increase loan assets by increasing deposits as liabilities out of nothing and increase their unearned interest revenues. So, the stock approach explains how banks can create credit money endogenously (FMC) (Jakab et al., 2014).

Schemmann (2013: 2) pointed out that:

> "This process of creating deposits as "cash in bank" does not comply with the Generally Accepted Accounting Principles (GAAP) or the International Financial Reporting Standards (IFRS). Furthermore, technically, it is not easy to differentiate deposits created under the flow and stock approaches explained above using the banking statistics" (Werner, 2015).

As long as deposits function as money, deposits and cash are used interchangeably in actual transactions as illustrated in Table A.3 below. For buyers and sellers in the non-banking public sector, the flow and stock approaches turn out to be indistinguishable on their balance sheets, in the sense that cash and deposits are in practice booked as the same Cash/Deposits account of assets[37].

---

37 In fact, cash and deposits items in many balance sheets are integrated as an inseparable Cash/Deposits stock.

Table A.3. Transactions of Non-Banking Sector: Stock Approach

Buyers		Sellers	
Debit (Assets)	Credit (Assets)	Debit (Assets)	Credit (Assets)
Commodity (+)	Deposits (-)	Deposits (+)	Commodity (-)
Commodity (+)	Cash (-)	Cash (+)	Commodity (-)

Chapter V
The Alternative System Design of
Public Money

Following the previous chapter, the alternative monetary system preventing monetary instabilities is fully explored in this chapter. The alternative system, based on the monetary reform of the Chicago Plan, is shown to attain monetary stability. As its by-product, debt liquidation of government is shown to be attained concurrently. Then, a business model of banks under the alternative system is briefly discussed in which banks become genuine intermediaries.

5.1 Revisiting Irving Fisher's 100 Percent Reserve Requirement Proposal:

The Great Depression in 1929 was the first major economic disaster caused by the system design failures of the debt money system. Faced with this design failure, eight economists at the University of Chicago[38] proposed an alternative system design called "The Chicago Plan for Banking Reform" in 1933 [4]. The plan was, then, vehemently carried on by Irving Fisher of Yale University (Fisher, 1935) and a group of

---

38 They were G.V. Cox, Aaron Director, Paul Douglas, A.G. Hart, F.H. Knight, L.W. Mints, Henry Schulz, and H.C. Simons. Their proposal was handed over, through Henry A. Wallace, Secretary of Agriculture, to the President Franklin D. Roosevelt on March 16, 1933. Unfortunately, it failed to be implemented. Instead, less restrictive Banking Act of 1933 to bankers, known as Glass-Steagal Act was legalized on June 16, 1933 (Phillips, 1995). The Act was repealed in 1999.

five economists[39] under the name "A Program for Monetary reform" (Fisher et al. 1939).

Their alternative system design was to introduce a required reserve ratio rule of 100 percent for demand deposits. The results of SD simulation are illustrative. Whenever a 100 percent reserve ratio is applied to a recessionary and unstable economic situation monetary behaviour gets, all of sudden, transformed into the stable (Figure 5.1).

Figure 5.1 100 percent reserve requirement rule introduced at t=10

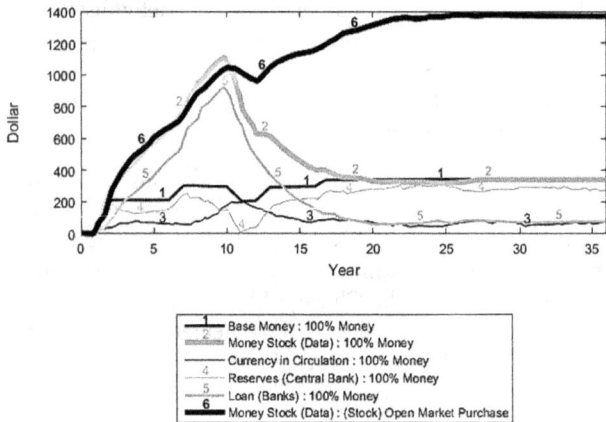

Instability of the money stock under a non-100 percent reserve ratio rule is perfectly subdued by the introduction of the

---

39 They are Paul H. Douglas, University of Chicago; Frank D. Graham, Princeton University; Earl J. Hamilton, Duke University; Willford I. King, New York University; and Charles R. Whittlesey, Princeton University.

full reserve rule so that base money (line 1) becomes identical to money stock (line 2). Theoretically, this can be easily confirmed as follows. When β = 1, we have m = 1 from Chapter 4 so that, assuming no vault cash held by banks, we have

Money Stock = m * High – Powerd Money = Base Money   [8]

Graphically, money multiplier (line 1) can be confirmed to converge to the value one as illustrated in Figure 5.2. Money convertibility coefficient (line 2) can be also demonstrated to converge to the value one, which implies that under the 100 % reserve money stock can be fully convertible to legal tender.

Under the full reserve system, functional-money disappears completely from the circulation and money stock becomes equal to legal tender (that is, base money). Accordingly, monetary stability is completely restored and money stock never gets affected by the changes in currency ratio and lending ratio, as well as repayment of loans.

Figure 5.2 Money Multiplier and Convertibility Coefficient under 100 percent Reserve Ratio

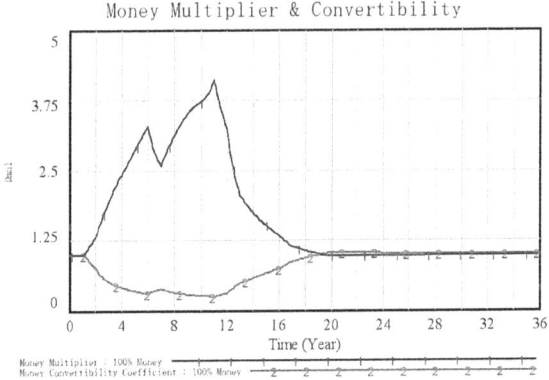

Money Multiplier : 100% Money
Money Convertibility Coefficient : 100% Money

Our SD simulation results confirm what Irving Fisher had proclaimed about a century ago:

> "I have come to believe that that plan, properly worked out and applied, is incomparably the best proposal ever offered for speedily and permanently solving the problem of depressions; for it would *remove the chief cause of both booms and depressions*, namely, the instability of demand deposits, tied as they are now, to bank loans." Fisher (1935: xviii; emphasis by the authors).

5.2 Public Money System

The mere introduction of a full reserve system is, it turns out, not enough to sustain ongoing economic activities, because money stock gets reduced from the previous level (line 6) to the base money level (line 1) as demonstrated in Figure 5.1. This shortage of money stock can be easily overcome by issuing new public money and putting it into circulation.

Who should create public money, then, in place of the central bank? Its issuer has to be a public organization, politically independent from the influences of the government and vested interest groups. At the same time, it should serve under the publicly elected legislative administrations, such as the parliament. Such an organization has been named as the *Public Money Administration* (PMA) in Yamaguchi (2013).[40]

Figure 3 illustrates how *public money* can be created by the public money administration (like central banks today) and put into government deposits accounts. Public money thus created simultaneously constitutes government equity, as well

---

40 Chapter 15 of his book compares system structures and behaviors of debt money and public money systems, and the next chapter 16 presents a generic transition process from the debt money system to the *public money* system. The specific transition process in Japan is proposed in Yamaguchi (2015).

as the assets of the PMA. Now the government gets ready to spend it through its public policies. The money so created can be spent on public infrastructure (education, IT, green energy, green transportation and health and social welfare programs). To make this alternative system design workable by avoiding political pressures to print more money, which causes inflation, the following two conditions have to be strictly met:

C1. The public money administration plays a role of *supply side* of public money, while the government (dept. of treasury or ministry of finance, etc.) plays a role of *demand side*. The amount of public money is determined by the interplay of the demand and supply sides.

C2. Transparency on the decision process going into the issuance of public money has to be guaranteed to the public.

Figure 5.3 Public Money into Circulation

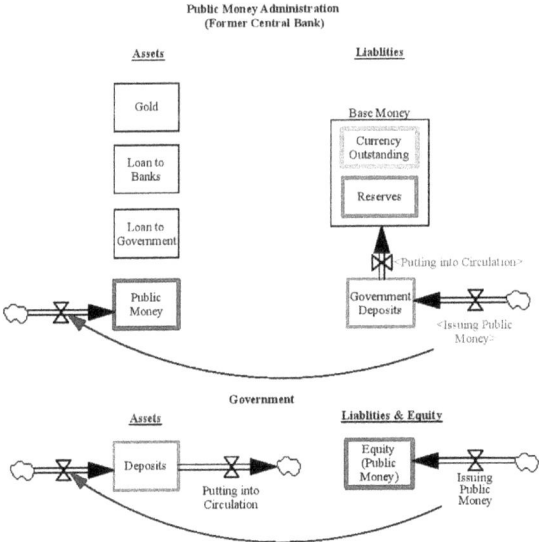

111

To see the results we ran a simulation. Adhering strictly to our model, we assume that $200 of public money is newly issued at t=18 for 5 years, totalling an input of $1,000. In this way, the original level of money stock (line 6) is restored as illustrated in Figure 5.4. If further money stock is needed for expanded economic activities, clearly more public money will be put into circulation through the above-mentioned issuance processes.

Yamaguchi (2013, Chapter 14) has provided additional results, based on his simulations of macroeconomic model with endogenous money creation. He has shown that debt-based money system generates more income inequality and shows unstable behaviors of economic growth and inflation compared to the proposed Public Money System.

Figure 5.4 Public Money Put into Circulation at t=18 for 5 years

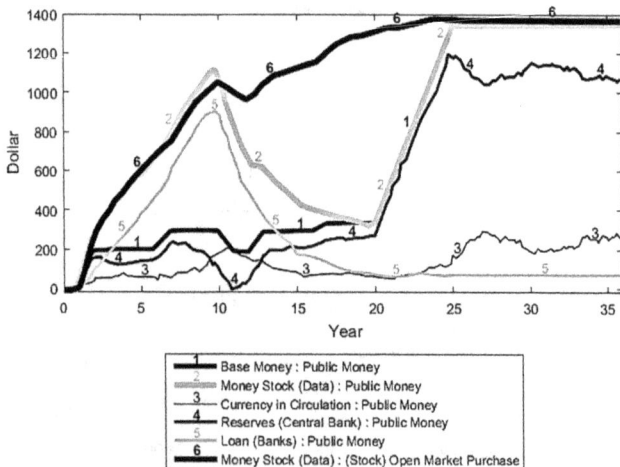

Base Money : Public Money
Money Stock (Data) : Public Money
3 — Currency in Circulation : Public Money
Reserves (Central Bank) : Public Money
5 — Loan (Banks) : Public Money
6 Money Stock (Data) : (Stock) Open Market Purchase

5.3 Government Debt Liquidation as a By-Product

Almost all the OECD countries are currently suffering from high public debt. Government debt has increased through fiscal policy implemented to save the slowdown in their economies caused by the system design failures. Accordingly, if the alternative system design can attain monetary stability, it should also be able to solve the debt problem. Indeed, Fisher argued that a 100 percent reserve can reduce government debt as follows:

> "(17) (b) As already noted, a *by-product* of the 100 % reserve system would be that *it would enable the Government gradually to reduce its debt*, through purchases of Government bonds by the Monetary Authority as new money was needed to take care of expanding business. Under the fractional reserve system any attempt to pay off the Government debt, whether by decreasing Government expenditures or by increasing taxation, threatens to bring about deflation and depression" Fisher (1939; emphasis by this authors).

It was already noted that in the 1930s neither austerity nor the policy of increased taxes, which caused deflation and depression, did not work to reduce government debt. Instead, we note that the 100 percent reserve system enables its reduction as its "by-product."

Figure 5.5 Framework of the Debt Liquidation Model

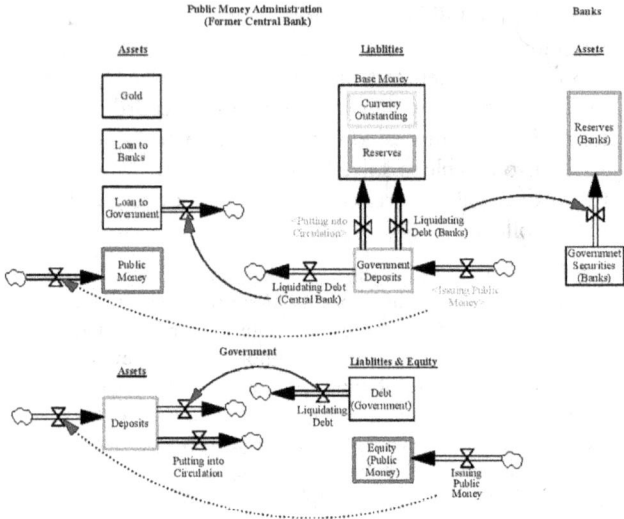

Let us investigate this assertion that debt liquidation works as a by-product of the full reserve system using a simulation exercise. Figure 5.5 provides our simplified modeling framework for liquidating debt. First, government securities held by the reformed central bank are redeemed directly from government deposits. Second, government securities held by commercial banks are purchased at book value by the public money administration, and sales revenues of the banks are used to secure their 100 % reserves of deposits. Third, government securities held by the public are purchased by the government through transactions via government deposits and bank reserves at the public money administration and public deposits at banks[41].

Such security purchases in turn guard against plausible risks to banks and the public that may be incurred by the enormous depreciation of security values, in case of financial crises and economic recessions. In addition, the alternative system design becomes a saver or a white knight for troubled banks, as well as the public. Let us assume in our model that debt liquidation under public money gets started at t=20 with a debt repayment period of 6 years. Figure 5.6 shows how government debt (line 1) is gradually liquidated. More specifically, debts held by the reformed central bank (line 2), by the banks (line 3) and by the public (line 4) are gradually liquidated[42].

Figure 5.6 Liquidating Debt

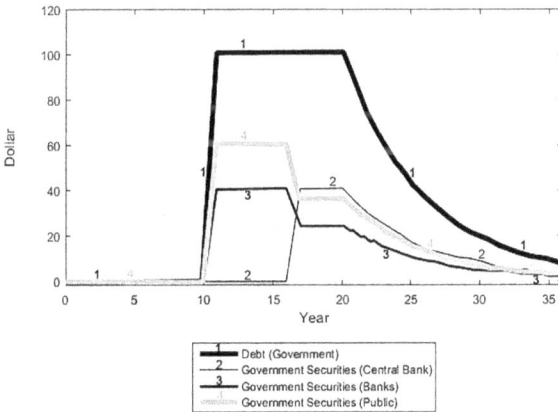

---

41 This transaction is not illustrated in the simplified Figure 5.

42 Debt liquidation issues are fully discussed in Chapters 12 and 13 of Yamaguchi (2015).

Through this process of debt liquidation, base money increases by $\Delta M0 = \$55.55$, which is used to liquidate the government securities held by the former central bank. The left-hand diagram of Figure 5.7 shows that the increase in public money stock through this debt liquidation, starting at t=20, is $\Delta M = \$47.6$. Base money and money stock will eventually be increased by the same amount when debt is completely liquidated.

Figure 5.7 Debt Liquidation under Full Reserve and
10 % Reserves

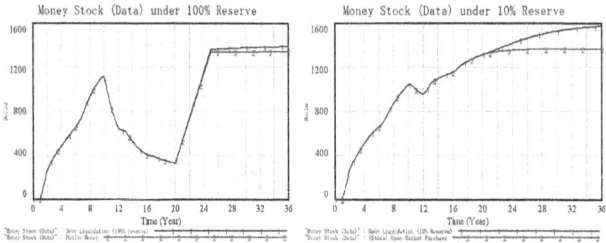

Government debt liquidation could also be carried out solely by issuing public money under the current fractional reserve system (10 % here). The right-hand panel of Figure 7 shows that the increase in money stock for this debt liquidation, starting at t=20, is $\Delta M = \$211.89$ due to the money multiplier effect. This forced liquidation, though it might work to reduce government debt, will surely cause hyper-inflation. This gives a serious warning to those who just propose government-issued money without introducing a 100 % reserve system. This implies that debt liquidation can be carried out most effectively under the public money system without causing inflation. Concurrently, as mentioned above, it could also be a white knight for troubled banks and the public.

116

5.4 Banks as Genuine Intermediaries

It can be argued that a genuine business model for banks would consist of service charges: under the 100 percent reserve requirement, commercial banks would be obliged to hold the full amount of customers' deposits. In consequence, the non-banking public sector can safely use their deposits anytime as legal tender for their transactions and economic activities. On the other hand, depositors have to pay service charges to the banks in exchange for these transaction services, like the present-day ATM service charges. These service charges in turn become a stable source of earned income for the banks. In this way, a robust and stable financial foundation will be established for the banking management.

As a by-product, banks no longer need to borrow or lend in the inter-bank money market. The inter-bank rate will no longer be applicable for borrowing or lending excess reserves to one another. As a result, the PMA (former central bank) will be free from complex market operations conducted daily under the current debt money system.

Earned Interest Income: If the full amount of deposits must be kept at banks, how can the banks find extra money for loans? Loanable funds for banks come from three sources: their own capital, repaid loans, and time deposits. Among these, time deposits will be a main source of loanable funds. Time deposits are nothing but the surplus deposits that are not needed for daily and short-term transactions, so that they are saved to the time deposits account.

In Figure 5.8, this process is illustrated as saving by the non-banking sectors, numbered (1), from their deposits to time deposits, and simultaneously the same amount of transfer takes place at banks. Banks are no longer obliged to keep these amounts of saving, which are then moved to their loanable funds from reserves. Banks now try to make loans to finance investments, numbered (2), out of their loanable funds, which become debts by the non-banking sector, numbered (3), as well as out of their deposits. Deposits at banks increase by the same amount, as well as their reserves. In this way, loans by banks out of loanable funds is balanced by their time deposits.

Figure 5.8 Public Money: Banks as Genuine Intermediaries

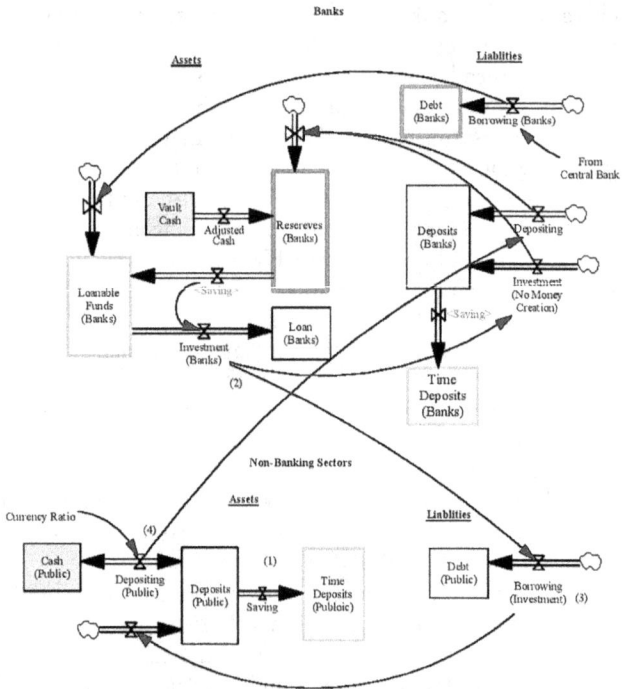

Accordingly, banks become efficient by offering higher interest rates for saving and lower interest for loans. Yet banks are no longer able to create functional-money at all, and become in this sense genuine intermediaries. Hence, their sources of loans are constantly limited to the available loanable fund, which is now legal tender.

Under these circumstances, bubbles and bursts can no longer occur, and existing financial markets are constrained to real zero-sum games; that is, losers and winners coexist. This implies that existing financial bonds and securities are no longer attractive to the banks as a whole. And loanable funds tend to be invested in the real economy from which positive interest revenues are obtained for banks as a whole, so long as the economy continues to grow.

In this way interest rates are competitively determined in the public money market, according to the available amount of saving and investment in the economy. Interest revenues thus obtained through arbitrage or the spread of lending and borrowing interest rates become truly their own earned income for the banks' efforts in providing investment banking services. Interest revenues, in this sense, are no longer unearned income out of nothing.

It is true that investment, whether real or financial, has been a risky economic activity through history. Accordingly, to avoid investment risks, earned interest income by banks from investment may be shared among banks and time deposits savers. This risk-sharing system has been historically developed as a "participatory banking" system under Islamic banking practices and a "mutual social financing" system known as Tanomoshi-kou in Japan since the 12th century.

Islamic banking finance is based on interest-free banking. The profit generated by means of loans is shared with the creditors. Meera and Larbani (2009) present their arguments against the creation of money under FMC as this is "creation of purchasing power out of nothing which brings about un-just transfers of assets in the economy." Islamic economists have been developing alternatives to the current system of banking. Anwar (1987) discusses a variety of options including a public money system of money creation and a banking system with 100 % reserve requirements.

5.6 Conclusions

Faced with the Great Depression in 1929 as a serious case of system design failure, a handful of American economists proposed an alternative design for the monetary reform system in the 1930s, the Chicago Plan. Its key pillar was the introduction of 100 percent required reserves in place of the fractional reserve banking system. Our SD model of the stock approach confirms that under the full reserve system monetary stability is fully attained, eliminating causes of booms and depressions. As a by-product, government debts are also gradually liquidated.

The modern version of this alternative system has been introduced as the *public money system*, under which a newly established "public money administration" is the sole issuer of public money for sustaining monetary stability, economic growth and social welfare.

Chapter VI
Conclusions and Some Free Thoughts on Money, Banking and Macroeconomics

During the Great Moderation (the period between the mid-1980s and 2007), the USA experienced unusual macroeconomic stability together with significant growth in asset prices and a shift in the distribution of credit to the financial and real estate sectors of the economy. In retrospect, this trend contributed to financial fragility; and, the bubble burst in 2007–2008. The crisis and the great recession that followed the crisis was an unexpected transition of the economy from one state to the other and caught many by surprise.

The mainstream macroeconomists had taken a benign view of the SMM prior to the crisis. The crisis made it clear that this view was mistaken, and a thorough and careful reassessment of the SMM is now warranted.

The crisis also highlighted some anomalies in the mainstream macroeconomic approach. An important one among them, discussed in this book, is the persistent and significant instability and decline in the velocity of money since the 1980s in most of the developed economies of the world. This renders the main conclusions of the quantity theory of money invalid.

Against this background, the book presents a critical review of the SMM approach as reflected in the family of DSGE models. It notes that, firstly, the approach has failed to capture the complex and dynamic nature of the monetary and financial sectors of the economy. Secondly, the role of banks, as portrayed in these models, does not conform to the views of many senior practitioners in central banks, specifically, results from empirical studies that present an entirely different view of the money creation process, the endogenous creation of money by banks (FMC). The ILF view in the mainstream models treats banks as mere financial intermediaries: as one person's (saver) spending goes down and another person's (borrower) spending goes up; this has, therefore, only distributional implications, and private debt and credit have no macroeconomic implications in these models.

The endogenous view of money can have useful insights in understanding the causes of the crisis and in resolving some of the anomalies. First, banks are not only creators of new liquidity, but they can also play a key role in its allocation. Second, money creation in this manner will add to the current aggregate demand, so that total spending will be the sum of income generated in the circular flow plus the net addition of debt for investment and consumption in the real sector of the economy [Keen, 2014b]. Once the endogenous creation of money by banks is taken into account, rising debt has macroeconomic implications as it adds to the aggregate demand (for example, use of credit cards and credit lines to business firms), and it opens those channels through which speculation on asset prices is financed. Credit flow to the financial sector can contribute to rising asset prices, capital gains becoming a function of aggregate financial credit creations. All these are not accounted for in the SMM, which weakens its explanatory power of the real world.

In the endogenous view of money, banks occupy a pivotal role in resolving some of the puzzling anomalies of macroeconomics. First, the decline in velocity of money, for example, led to the breakdown of the money demand function. One of the explanations of this persistent decline can be explained by the allocations of credit to non-real sector transactions. These flows are not accounted for in the quantity theory of money equation. It has been shown empirically that credit flows for real sector transactions can significantly explain nominal growth in GDP, including in the US and in Japan.

Second, the endogenous credit growth to finance transactions in the financial markets can also explain asset price bubbles. The role of "Ponzi financiers" in Minsky's explanation of the bursting of the bubble and the ensuing great recession can also be explained by this very critical role of the banks. Third, the lack of effectiveness of post-crisis monetary policy prescriptions in recent years and during the lost decades of Japan in the 1990s can also be linked to the limitations of the mainstream macroeconomic model where money is assumed to be exogenous and private debt has no macroeconomic implications. With the endogenous view of money and the dynamics of balance sheet recession, however, the failure of the extraordinary expansion in base money through quantitative easing and the zero-bound interest rate can be explained.

There are both long and short term policy implications that can be drawn from our discussions. Our discussion also provokes some free thoughts on research relating to money, banking and macroeconomics. These are enumerated below.

1. Monitoring and regulating the credit and asset markets should become part of macroprudential policy. Trends in asset prices and credit flows that support the activities of the monetary and financial sector (finance, insurance and real estate) can provide critical information about the state of financial fragility and should be subject to macroprudential regulations (Claudio, 2012). Researchers at the Bank of International Settlements have been calling for attention to the developments in the assets markets and to financial stability. They were calling for regulations even prior to the crisis (Bezemer and Grydaki, 2014). Godley and Wray (2000) were able to predict the crisis by using accounting methods.

2. Flow-of-funds analysis can be used to quantify the sustainability of debt burden and the financial sector's drain

on the real economy. The data on financial flows is now available in many advanced and emerging economies. The economy's assets and liabilities must balance; excessive growth in financial asset markets is therefore reflected in growing debt burden. This helps foresee trends in the financial sector in relation to the real sector and assess if these trends are sustainable in the future or not. This suggests that the inclusion of indicators of financial fragility based on accounting methods can complement conventional macroeconomic policy analysis.

3. Recent empirical research has supported the important role played by banks in allocating credit to the real sector for productive purposes (Werner, 2011). Buyukkarabacak and Krause (2009) have shown, for example, that in Germany during 1933–1960s, directing credit to the real sector, while severely limiting its flows to speculation and consumption, played a critical role in economic development and stability, and thus the prevention of crises. It can be argued that the economic "control" in Germany still continues. The policies in Germany still favor manufacturing and the real sector. Perhaps as a consequence, real estate bubbles have not occurred in Germany, although the growth and productivity performance of the German economy has been quite successful, both before and after the global crisis. Nevertheless, given these restrictions and in search of high profits, many German banks tended to place their funds out of the country, for example, in real estate financing in Turkey and Greece, or investing in or marketing US subprime securities. The latter, the subprime bonds, were the main conduit of the US financial crisis into Europe; recently, in 2016, US regulators heavily fined (USD 14 billion) Deutsche Bank for its sales of faulty American mortgage-based securities prior to the global crisis.

4. Similarly, the "East Asian Economic Miracle" has been attributed by some to the interventions in credit markets through central bank "window guidance," interventions in the interest rates, and directed credit.[43] The credit flow to sectors with higher value-added potential had been encouraged and credit for speculative or consumption purposes was repressed. The Bank of England (BoE) has recently embarked on a policy of managing bank lending under the "Funding for Lending Scheme," which directs credit to SMEs (Lyonnet, and Werner (2012)). The credit guidance principles are not necessarily based on principles of the command economy. Rather, they can be based on the fundamentals of market economies with private ownership, but not relying entirely on assumptions based on the microeconomic behaviours of economic agents as in SMM approach.

5. There is still too much reliance on the theoretical models that omit the financial sector. Private debt levels are still very high after the crisis and make the financial system financially fragile. The annual report of BIS has again warned about it in its 2014 report. They are however, also not well incorporated in the SMM. There is a need to search for alternative paradigm(s) where financial markets and the role of banks can be effectively modelled. Inclusion of the financial market in the formulation of the macroeconomic policies towards stable growth is of paramount importance.

6. Islamic Finance, revived since the early 1970s, has proven more resilient in withstanding the financial crisis and is also better equipped to prevent the materializing of crisis as well. Islamic economic principles are based on

---

43 See Yülek (1997).

the pillar of "profit and loss sharing;" having the right to profit also implies equally sharing the risk of incurring loss. The prior consent to share the risks along with profits increases the stability of the system and prevents excessive lending. The transformation of the Islamic financial paradigm into a viable system for today's complicated economic relations is an evolutionary process. However, some of the governing modes of finance that are being practiced by Islamic banks, such as *Murahaba*, *Mudaraba* and *Musharaka* do link the loans to activities in the real economy and avoid financing speculative investments.

7. We presented the ASD (Accounting System Dynamics) approach in explaining the process of the endogenous creation of money, using balance sheet accounting. This also highlights the system design failure(s) of the current financial system (the debt-money based system) using system dynamics modeling and conclusions drawn from the Japanese economy. ASD modeling has also been employed to design a system based on the key recommendations of the Chicago Plan with 100 % reserve requirements. The results of model show that the system under the Chicago Plan does become more stable and its implementation by-product, liquidation of government debt, is also shown to be attained concurrently.

8. A 100 % reserve requirement proposal may seem farfetched and revolutionary in nature. However, it would restrain banks from creating money endogenously. DSGE models failed in predicting the crisis and explaining the anomalies, as they could not model the banks and financial sectors appropriately or adequately. Reforming the system on the basis of 100 % reserves will, in fact, render the DSGE model useful for macro policy prescriptions. Then reality will start to function like the model's

assumptions. So one either needs to reform the banking system in line with the recommendations of the Chicago Plan or to search for an alternative model that is based on more realistic assumptions about endogenous money and the dynamics of financial sector.

9. There has been significant progress in developing macro models based on the SFC (Stock Flow Consistent) approach in recent years. For example, Godley and Lavoie (2007) have recently laid down good foundations for the development of models based on the SFC approach. Keen (2013) and Bezemer (2012) have also developed SD models in which they have shown the vulnerability of the current monetary system based on the endogenous view of money. Yamaguchi & Yamaguchi (2016) have provided details of their proposal for a public money system with a 100 % reserve requirement.

10. The failure of the policy prescriptions based on traditional models in the current post-crisis scenario and their inability to avoid the lost decades of Japan pose major challenges to the current state of macroeconomics. Developing models with more realistic views of the financial sectors, particularly the banking sector, may warrant a major shift in the axiomatic foundations of the current paradigm. The ideological vision based on the notions of equilibrium and rational choice by optimizing agents may need to be scrutinized, particularly with reference to the role played by Ponzi financiers and speculators in contributing to the financial fragility of the system. This may suggest the importance of devising a more effective regulatory framework.

These concerns have recently been echoed in the concluding comments on the future of macroeconomic policy (posted on IMF direct, 2011), by Oliver Blanchard. First, macro policymaking has entered into a new brave world.

Second, in the age-old discussion of the relative roles of markets and state, the pendulum has swung towards the state. Third, the crisis has shown that many distortions within the world of finance had been ignored, thinking they were the domain of microeconomics; now it is being realized that they are also macro-relevant. Finally, monetary policy has to go beyond inflation stability, adding output and financial stability to the list of its targets.

References

Allen, F. & Gale, D. (2000). Bubbles and crisis. *The Economic Journal 110*, 236–235.

Ang, J. (2008). A survey of recent developments in the literature of finance and growth. *Journal of Economic Surveys*, 22: 536–76.

Anwar, M. (1987). Reorganization of Islamic banking: a new proposal. *American Journal of Islamic Social Sciences*, 4(2), 295.

Arcand, J. L., Berkes, E. & Panizza, U. (2012). Too much finance? IMF *Working Paper* No. 161.

Arestis, P. & Sawyer, M. (2002, September). *Can monetary policy affect the real economy?* Levy Economics Institute of Bard College, Sept. 2002. (*Working Paper*, n. 355).

Aschheim, J. (1959). Commercial banks and financial intermediaries: fallacies and policy implications. *The Journal of Political Economy*, pp. 59–71.

Baker, D., DeLong, J. B. & Krugman, P. R. (2005). Asset returns and economic growth. Brookings *Papers on Economic Activity*, *2005*(1), 289–330.

Bank of England (2014, Q1). Money creation in the modern economy, by Michael McLeay, Amar Radia and Ryland Thomas of the Bank's Monetary Analysis Directorate, *Quarterly Bulletin*, Q1 2014.

Beck, T. *et al.* (2012). *Financial innovations: the bright and the dark sides.* SSRN *Working Paper.*

Benes, J. & Kumhof, M. (2012). *The Chicago Plan revisited*, WP/12/202. Washington DC: IMF.

Bernanke, Ben. (2000). *Essays on the Great Depression.* Princeton: Princeton University Press.

Bernanke, Ben. (2004, February). The Great Moderation. At the meeting of the Eastern Economic Association, Washington, D.C., February 20.

Bernanke, Ben. (2010). On the implications of the financial crisis for economics. Conference Co-sponsored by the Center for Economic Policy Studies and Bendheim Center for Finance, Princeton University. Princeton, NJ: US Federal Reserve.

Bezemer, D. J. (2011). *Causes of financial instability: don't forget finance.* Levy Economics Institute of Bard College *Working Paper.* (665).

Bezemer, D. J. (2010). Understanding financial crisis through accounting models. *Accounting, Organizations and Society, 35*(7), 676–688.

Bezemer, D. J. & Grydaki,M. (2014). Financial fragility in the Great Moderation. *Journal of Banking & Finance, 49,* 169–177.

Bezemer, D. J. (2014). Schumpeter might be right again: the functional differentiation of credit. *Journal of Evolutionary Economics, 24*(5), 935–950.

Blanchard, O. & Simon, J. (2001). The long and large decline in U.S. output volatility. Brookings *Papers on Economic Activity 1,* 135–164.

Blanchard, Olivier (2008, August). *The state of macro.* National Bureau of Economic Research (NBER); Peter G. Peterson Institute for International Economics, August 12.

Blanchard, O. and Dell'Ariccia. (2010). Rethinking macroeconomic policy. *Journal of Money Credit and Banking, 42,* 199–215.

Blanchard, O. (2014). How the crisis changed macroeconomics, *VoxEu.*

Boughton, J. M. (1991). Long-run money demand in large industrial countries. *Staff Papers, 38*(1), 1–32. IMF.

Brown, J. (2015). *Chart o'day: the (non) velocity of money*. False Courage, CSLA, http://thereformedbroker. com/2015/10/08/chart-o-the-day-the-non-velocity-of-money/

Bundesbank (2009). *Geld und Geldpolitik*. Frankfurt: Deutsche Bundesbank.

Caverzasi, E. & Godin, A. (2013). *Stock flow: consistent modelling through the ages. Working Paper Series 745.* The Levy Economics Institute of Bard College.

Cecchetti, S. & Kharroubi, E. (2012). Reassessing the impact of finance on growth. BIS *Working Papers* No. 381.

Claudio B. (2012, December) *The financial cycle and macroeconomics: what have we learnt? Working Paper* No. 395, Bank for International Settlements, December 2012.

Copeland, M. (1949, July). Social accounting for money flows. *The Accounting Review, 24*:3, 254–264 .

Davis, J. & Kahn, James. (2008, July). *Interpreting the Great Moderation: changes in the volatility of economic activity at the macro and micro levels, Staff Report* no. 334, Federal Reserve Bank of New York, July 2008.

Eggertsson, G. B. & Krugman, P. (2012). Debt, deleveraging, and the liquidity trap: a Fisher-Minsky-Koo approach. *The Quarterly Journal of Economics*, *127*(3), 1469–1513.

Fagiolo, G. & Roventini, A. (2012). Macroeconomic policy in DSGE and agent-based models. *Revue de l'OFCE*, (5), 67–116.

Fisher, I. (1945). *100 % money: designed to keep checking banks 100 % liquid; to prevent inflation and deflation; largely to cure or prevent depressions: and to wipe out much of the national debt. New York: Adelphi Publishing.*

Douglas, P. H. *et al.* (1939). *A program for monetary reform.* Available at faculty.chicagobooth.edu/amir.sufi/research/MonetaryReform_1939.pdf.

Friedman, M. (1987). Monetary policy: tactics versus strategy: the search for stable money, pp. 361–82. Essays on Monetary reform, Chicago/London: University of Chicago Press.

Friedman, Milton. (1960). *A program for monetary stability. New York: Fordham University Press.*

Fullwiler, S. T. (2013, Summer). An endogenous money perspective on the post-crisis monetary policy debate. *Review of Keynesian Economics,* 1:2, 171–194.

Galbraith, John Kenneth. (1955). *The Great Crash 1929.* Boston: Houghton Mifflin Company.

Gali, J. and Gambetti, L. (2009) On the sources of the Great Moderation. *American Economic Journal: Macroeconomics* 2009 1:1, 26–57

Godley, W. & Lavoie, M. (2007). *Monetary economics.* Hampshire: Palgrave Macmillan.

Godley, W. & Shaikh, A. (2002). An important inconsistency at the heart of the Standard Macroeconomic Model. *Journal of Post Keynesian Economics,* 24:3, 423–443.

Godley, W. & Wray, L. R. (2000). Is Goldilocks doomed? *Journal of Economic Issues,* 34(1), 201–206.

Godley, W. & Zezza, G. (2006). *Debt and lending: a* cri de coeur. Levy Institute at Bard College *Policy Notes 2006/4.*

Goldfeld, S. M. & Sichel, D. E. (1990). The demand for money. *Handbook of monetary economics,* 1, 299–356.

Goldsmith, R. (1969). *Financial structure and development.* New Haven: Yale University Press.

Goodhart, C. (1989). The conduct of monetary policy. *The Economic Journal,* 99(396), 293–346.

Goodwin, Richard. (1967). A growth cycle," in C. H. Feinstein (ed.), *Socialism, capitalism and economic growth*. Cambridge: Cambridge University Press, pp. 54–58.

Guttentag, J. M. & Lindsay, R. (1968, Sept.-Oct.). The uniqueness of commercial banks. *Journal of Political Economy*, 76(5), 991–1014.

Gurley, J. G. & Shaw, E.S. (1955). Financial aspects of economic development. *American Economic Review*, 45, 515–528.

Hahn, L. A. (1924). *Volkswirtschaftliche Theorie des Bankkredits*. Tübingen: Mohr, 2nd Edition. Hudson, M. (2006). The road to serfdom: an illustrated guide to the coming real estate collapse. *Harper's Magazine*.

Jakab Z. & Kumhof, M. (2015, May). Banks are not intermediaries of loanable funds and why this matters, *Working Paper* No. 529, Bank of England, May, 2015.

Jappelli T., Pagano, M. & Maggio, M. (2008, November). Households' indebtedness and financial fragility. Paper presented at the 9th Jacques Polak Annual Research Conference, hosted by the International Monetary Fund, November 13–14, 2008.

Jordà, O., Schularick, M. & Taylor, A. (2011). When credit bites back: leverage, business cycles, and crises. Federal Reserve Bank of San Francisco *Working Paper Series* No. 2011–27.

Keen, S. (1995). Finance and economic breakdown: modelling Minsky's Financial Instability Hypothesis. *Journal of Post Keynesian Economics*, 17(4)4, 607–635.

Keen, S. (2009). The dynamics of the monetary circuit, in *The political economy of monetary circuits*. Palgrave Macmillan UK, pp. 161–187.

Keen, S. (2011). Economic growth, asset markets and the credit accelerator. *Real-World Economics Review*, *57*, 25–40.

Keen, S. (2014a). Secular stagnation and endogenous money. *Real-World Economics Review*, *66*, 2–11.

Keen, S. (2014b). Endogenous money and effective demand. *Review of Keynesian Economics*, *2*(3), 271–291.

Keen, S. (2013). A monetary Minsky model of the Great Moderation and Great Recession. *Journal of Economic Behaviour & Organization*, *86*, 221–235.

Keydland, F.E. & Prescott, E.C. (1990) Business cycles: real facts and a monetary myth. Federal Reserve Bank of Minneapolis *Quarterly Review*, *14*:2, 3–18.

King, G.R. & Levine, R. (1993). Finance and growth: Schumpeter might be right. *The Quarterly Journal of Economics*, *108*, 717–37

Kohn, M. (1988). *The finance constraint theory of money: a progress report*. The Jerome Levy Economics Institute Working Paper, (5).

Koo, R. (2011). The world in balance sheet recession: causes, cure, and politics. Real-world economics review, 58(12), 19–37.

Koo, R. (2016). *Authorities and markets continue to ignore real economy and act on textbook assumptions,* Tokyo: Nomura Research Institute.

Krugman, Paul. (2009). How did economists get it so wrong? *New York Times*, September 2.

Krugman, P. & Eggertsson, G. B. (2011). Debt, deleveraging and the liquidity trap. In *2011 Meeting Papers* (No. 1166). Society for Economic Dynamics.

Leijonhufvud, J. (2009). *Macroeconomics and the crisis, a personal appraisal*. London: Centre for Economic Policy Research Policy Insight.

Lietaer, Bernard A. *et al.* (2012). *Money and sustainability: the missing link*. Axminster UK: Triarchy Press, chapters VII and VIII.

LSE. (2011). Getting in shape: leveraging our assets, developing opportunities. *Annual Report*, London, Stock Exchange Group.

Lucas, Robert E. Jr. (2003). Macroeconomic priorities. *American Economic Review*, *93*, 1–14.

Lyonnet, V. & Werner, R. (2012). Lessons from the Bank of England on 'quantitative easing' and other 'unconventional' monetary policies. *International Review of Financial Analysis*, *25*, 94–105.

Macleod, H. D. (1894). *The theory of credit*, vol. 2. London: Longmans, Green.

Mankiw, N. G. (2006). The macroeconomist as scientist and engineer. *The Journal of Economic Perspectives, 20*(4), 29–46.

McLeay, M., Radia, A. & Thomas, R. (2014, Q1). Money creation in the modern economy. Bank of England *Quarterly Bulletin*, Q1.

Meera, A. K. M. & Larbani, M. (2009). Seigniorage of fiat money and the Maqāsid al-Sharī'ah: the unattainableness of the Maqāsid. In AK Meera, *Real Money*, pp. 1–34.

Minsky, H. (1978). The financial instability hypothesis: a restatement. *Thames Papers on Political Economy*.

Minsky, Hyman. (1982). *Can "it" happen again?: essays on instability and finance*. Armonk, NY: M.E. Sharpe.

Moore, B. (2006). *Shaking the invisible hand: complexity, endogenous money and exogenous interest rates*. Springer-Verlag Berlin and Heidelberg GmbH & Co.

Moore, B. J. (2001). Some reflections on endogenous money. In *Credit, interest rates and the open economy: essays on horizontalism*, pp. 11. Cheltenham and Northampton: Edward Elgar. Moore, B. J. (1979). The endogenous money stock. *Journal of Post Keynesian Economics, 2*:1, 49–70.

RBA (2008, December). Interesting times. Speech by Glenn Stevens, Governor of the Reserve Bank of Australia, to the Australian business economists' annual dinner, Sydney, 9 December 2008. <http://www.rba.gov.au/Speeches/2008/sp_gov_091208.html>.

Reinhart, C. M. & Rogoff, K. S. (2009). *This time it's different: eight centuries of financial folly*. Princeton: Princeton University Press.

Rossouw, J. (2014). Private shareholding and public interest: an analysis of an eclectic group of central banks (No. 457). ERSA, Cape Town, SA. Rousseau, P. & Wachtel, P. (2011). What is happening to the impact of financial deepening on economic growth? *Economic Inquiry, 49*, 276–88.

Samuelson, P. (1948). *Economics*. New York: McGraw-Hill.

Schumpeter, J. (1934). *The theory of economic development*. Cambridge: Harvard University Press.

Shaw, E. (1973). *Financial deepening and economic development*. New York: Oxford University Press.

Shirakawa, M. (2008). *Modern monetary policy in theory and practice*. Tokyo: Nihon Keizai.

Smith, P. F. (1966). The concepts of money and commercial banks. *Journal of Finance, 21*(4), 635–648.

Snowdon, B. & Vane, H. R. (2005). *Modern macroeconomics: its origins, development and current state*. Northampton, MA: Edward Elgar Publishing.

Solow, R. (2010). Testimony to Congress given to the House Committee on Science and Technology.

Stiglitz, Joseph E. (2011). Rethinking macroeconomics: what failed, and how to repair it. *Journal of European Economic Association* 9(4): 591–645.

Stock, J. H. & Watson W. (2002). Has the Business Cycle Changed and Why, *NBER Macroeconomics Annual 2000*. National Bureau of Economic Research, Inc., pp 159–230.

Stone, C. & Thornton D. L. (1987, August/September). *Solving the 1980s' velocity puzzle: a progress report*. Federal Reserve Bank of St. Louis, August/September 1987.

Tovar, C. (2008). DSGE models and central banks. Bank of International Settlements, Monetary and Economic Department *Working Paper* no. 28. Basel: BIS.

Tobin, J. (1963). Commercial banks as creators of money. Cowles Foundation Paper 205, reprinted in D. Carson (ed.), *Banking and Monetary Studies*. Homewood, IL: Richard D. Irwin.

Tobin, J. (1984). On the efficiency of the financial system. Lloyds Bank *Annual Review* (153), pp. 1–15.

Turner, A. (2010). What do banks do? Why do credit booms and busts occur and what can public policy do about it? *The Future of Finance*, 5: LSE Report. London: London School of Economics and Political Science.

Vivian, R. W. & Spearman, N. (2015). Some clarity on banks as financial intermediaries and money "creators" (No. 523). Working paper, Johannesburg, South Africa: School of Economic and Business Services, University of the Witwatersrand.

Werner, R. A. (1993). Japanese capital flows: did the world suffer from yen illusion? Toward a quantity theory of disaggregated credit. In the Proceedings of the Annual Conference of the Royal Economic Society, London.

Werner, R. A. (1997). Towards a new monetary paradigm: a quantity theorem of disaggregated credit, with evidence from Japan. *Kredit und Kapital, 30*(2), 276–309.

Werner, R. A. (2005). *New paradigm in macroeconomics* (Vol. 213). Basingstoke: Palgrave Macmillan.

Werner, R. (2011). Economics as if banks mattered: a contribution based on the inductive methodology. *The Manchester School, 79*(s2), 25–35.

Werner, R. A. (2012). Towards a new research programme on 'banking and the economy'—Implications of the Quantity Theory of Credit for the prevention and resolution of banking and debt crises. *International Review of Financial Analysis, 25*, 1–17.

Werner, R. A. (2014). How do banks create money, and why can other firms not do the same? An explanation for the coexistence of lending and deposit-taking. *International Review of Financial Analysis, 36*, 71–77,

Werner, R. A. (2015). A lost century in economics: three theories of banking and the conclusive evidence. *International Review of Financial Analysis.*

Wicksell, K. (1898). *Geldzins und Güterpreise. Eine Untersuchung über die den Tauschwert des Geldes bestimmenden Ursachen.* Jena: Gustav Fischer (tr., 1936. *Interest and prices: a study of the causes regulating the value of money.* London: Macmillan).

Withers, H. (1916). Business of finance. London: Smith, Eldet & Co. Xu Hailiang (2011). *Macroeconomics after the great recession: consensus or conflict?* Electronic thesis and Dissertation paper 720, Graduate Studies, University of Denver, USA.

Withers, H. (1921). *The meaning of money* (Vol. 2). New York: EP Dutton and Company.

Yamaguchi, K. (2013). Accounting System Dynamics approach. Japan Futures Research Center, Osaka Office (Publication).

Yamaguchi, K. & Yamaguchi, Y. (2016). Head and tail of money creation and its system design failures, Working Paper, Japan Futures Research Centre, Osaka, Japan. Yulek, M. A. (1997). Financial repression in Japan during the high growth period (1953–73). *METU Studies in Development, 24*, 575–595.

Zarlenga, S. (2002). *The lost science of money: the mythology of money, the story of power*. Valatie. New York: American Monetary Institute.

Subject Index

Name Index

www.ingramcontent.com/pod-product-compliance
Lightning Source LLC
Chambersburg PA
CBHW071747270326
41928CB00013B/2826